NOD HOUSE

ALSO BY NATHANIEL MACKEY

Poetry Books and Chapbooks

Four for Trane
Septet for the End of Time
Outlantish
Song of the Andoumboulou: 18-20
Four for Glenn
Eroding Witness
School of Udhra
Whatsaid Serif
Splay Anthem

Fiction

Bedouin Hornbook
Djbot Baghostus's Run
Atet A.D.
Bass Cathedral
From a Broken Bottle Traces of Perfume Still Emanate: Vols. 1–3

Criticism

Discrepant Engagement: Dissonance, Cross-Culturality, and
*   Experimental Writing*
Paracritical Hinge: Essays, Talks, Notes, Interviews

Anthologies

Moment's Notice: Jazz in Poetry and Prose, with Art Lange

Recordings

Strick: Song of the Andoumboulou 16-25

NOD HOUSE

NATHANIEL MACKEY

A NEW DIRECTIONS BOOK

Some of these poems first appeared in the following publications: *AMER-
ARCANA: A Bird & Beckett Review, Bay Poetics, Call: Review, Callaloo, Cavalier
Literary Couture, Chicago Review, Conjunctions, Front Porch, The Gig, Hambone,
Marsh Hawk Review, The Nation, 1913: A Journal of Forms, No: A Journal of the
Arts, Ocho, Quarterly West, Talisman,* and *Verse.*

Manufactured in the United States of America
New Directions Books are printed on acid-free paper.
First published as a New Directions Paperbook (NDP1216) in 2011
Published simultaneously in Canada by Penguin Books Canada Limited

Library of Congress Cataloging-in-Publication Data
Mackey, Nathaniel, 1947–
Nod house / Nathaniel Mackey.
p. cm.
Poems.
ISBN 978-0-8112-1946-4 (pbk. : alk. paper)
I. Title.
PS3563.A3166N63 2011
811'.5—dc22

                    2011018430

10 9 8 7 6 5 4 3 2 1

New Directions Books are published for James Laughlin
by New Directions Publishing Corporation
80 Eighth Avenue, New York, NY 10011

for my brother
Richard Mackey

CONTENTS

I. QUAG

II. QUAG

where nothing native belongs
and all is figure and blindness
—Jay Wright, *Music's Mask and Measure*

to smoke out thoughts of home
—Ted Pearson, *Catenary Odes*

I

QUAG

SOUND AND SOMNOLENCE

—"mu" fortieth part—

A light, floating slumber
it seemed. Buoyant heads,
  we lay like melons, the
pond our melon patch,
                bobbed,
  kept endlessly afloat...
  Risen waft, anabatic
            whiff.
Buried heads brought back
  to life... Buried our heads in
    Erzulie's loin-musk, imagined
    more than real, all the more
                penetrant,
  punishment the moon doled out...
We awoke blinking, blinded by
    the water's wry perfume. Blinked
  and blinked. Blinked. Blinked
             and
    blinked again, bobbing heads
    up to our noses in water, the
pond a pool of reflection gone
             dark...
  It was a dream we were hounded
by, Erzulie's frog-princes yet to
  be kissed... We'd have blown
    ourselves up and the world
            as
  well so exhausted we were, all a
banality, all the world in one boat...
  Nubs what were fingers at arm's
    end, only knuckles to hold on
  with. What we wanted withdrew,
            ab-
stract assembly, said we'd someday
meet among rocks... Run brethren
    obsessed with Erzulie, recollecting
    her perfumed inner thigh. Aroma
            we'd

have given an arm to draw the likes
of, synaesthetic brush, bouquet. Risen
　　scent, given our wish, would lift
us, an expended we underlay all
else. "Love's made bed my hounfour,"

　　　　　　　　　　　　　　　　she'd
　　say, "love's bed Agwé's boat."

　　　　　　　　　　　　　　Wafted
　　aroma translated had us up to our
mouths in water, pond water up to
　　one's upper lip. Insecure hold on
where one was, nose above water,

　　　　　　　　　　　　　　　love's
amphibious hush… Though it was
　　land we were on, stomachs in our
throats, scared, not-right-if-not-scared
no solace, better to be wrong we

　　　　　　　　　　　　thought…

　　Or so we thought, said we thought,
　　laughed as we spoke, smoke rings
floated, we were Dread Lakes eldren,
　　soapwater cigarette smoke… Smoke
　　bubbles lifted our lungs up our throats,

　　　　　　　　　　　　　　　　it
wasn't virgin earth we were on. Nothing
　　lay north, no way to keep our feet. Crept
and kept falling, fell, got up again, Crab

　　　　　　　　　　　　　　Alley
　　lay to our left. Abrupt falling off of the
earth to our right, everything lay to our
　　left… A frog pond aperture it was we
looked in thru, synaesthetic mingling of

　　　　　　　　　　　　　　mud
　　and perfume, not-yet princes yet to be
　　kissed, fairy tale yet to come true… Our
princess would come someday, soon come,
　　prophecy said as much… Dread Lakes' dry

　　　　　　　　　　　　　　bed
　　the bed we lay with Erzulie in, a slow song
　　song even so. So slow sing was less what

we did than survive it, frogs in a nearby
                                        pond
    infiltrating sleep, a bit of something heard
                                            before
        dozing

We saw light, sought shadow we
thought we saw. We saw our heads
roll away whatever we saw… We
were again at the foot of a ladder,
                                broken
    rung where we stepped everywhere
we stepped, rung we'd have bounded
from. We were going nowhere, step
    stayed with us, callipygian Erzulie
no longer held sway… Sisyphean
                                heads
hard as rocks rolled up, slid back down…
Trudged up Treadnot Hill… Step
stuck to our feet even so, we dragged
    it with us, a dream we dreamt we
                                dreamt
    laid to rest. The ravening horns were
                                at
our backs, we hung our heads, wilted
lilies, bells holding more than was there.
    Step stood in our way, we were running
    in place,   world and wear synonymous,
        rung and retraction one… Rung lay
                                wasted,
    lift lay as well, rayed-out gallows the ground
        had become, abstract ascendancy's drop…
    What remained of rung we were loath to
        say. Chime. Climb. Clime. Clamor. Claim
                                we
        absconded
        with

•

Bodiless heads alive bobbing in water.
So innocent seeming, what did it
mean? Mine alone it began but grew,
                              more
heads appeared,   melon-patch appre-
    hension, heads would roll...
                              Tumble-
weeds we'd have been were it not a
melon patch we were in, a frog pond
even so. Had already rolled, were already
                              rolling...
We'd lost our heads it wanted to say, lost
to the world, Erzulie's remnant perfume.
Sound where before we'd have said soul,
    so much less ensouled of late. So much
                              less
    if not overly so, we lay corrected, heads
held elsewhere, hit... World old and we
    with it, new could we awake, deep
        sleep deeper the more we resisted,
        quicksand it seemed we were in...
                              Shook
    loose though, ascended like balloons.
What it was was only atmosphere, air,
    an imagined incense, heads up in clouds
of smoke. We floated on air, heads lighter
                              than
        air,   looked out on where we other-
    wise were... Pool, pond, pole it now
                              seemed,
    reed blown on by lips rippling water,
wind we were lifted by... Rather one's head
on Erzulie's lap than head of state, rather
make love than war. So went the slogan,
        placards held high,   rallied, spoke
                              with our
        feet... March our birthright, year after year,
    centuries-long trek we were on. Stilt what'd
        been stake, stuck, stutter, stalk we were
                              hoisted

by… The exemplary two turned impossible,
back where they'd been before, blue fingers
rummaging bulge and recess… Lost heads.
Greek absurdities… Rolled up only to roll
                                    back
down… Rumbling heads apart from headless
bodies, bodies and heads up against a wall…
    Said again we'd sit in Squat Garden, bottom-
heavy body, bottom-heavy soul,   rolled
    heads' melon-patch epiphany's bone patch,
                                        birds
    fly away from our bleeding lips… Kissed
out, my late head lay compressed and
    compounded, beginning to be a ghost,
                                        gray
    sidehair, gray goatee… Down a slope known
    as Down the Hill   were kids again,
                                    crouched
catching tadpoles, awoke to
roll back
down

No daydream was it, no afternoon of
　a Georgia faun though we were
　　in Georgia. Athens it turned out we
　　were in... Words' rescue no rescue,
　　　　　　　　　　　　cracked
　voices backed by intransigent hum, what
　　we knew was only we'd been hit... Night
　　birds, frogs, tree frogs, crickets, an
　aleatory orchestra it seemed. Wooed
by which, resisting which, totemic,
　　　　　　　　　　We
lay on our backs' reconnoiter's ninety-
　　degree drift. Erzulie was Our Lady, Our
　Lady's hips our pillow, the pond's banks the
backs of her thighs... We stood on our feet as
　　　　　　　　　　　though
　　we lay on our backs, devices bare, awaiting,
not know-how, gnosis, albeit neither repaid our wait...
　　We stood without backs, without bodies, bodies
below water, heads moored, bobbing on the face
　　　　　　　　　　　　of the
　　water, heads between Our Lady's legs... Orphic
　　loss taken in thru an acoustic window, black gnostic
　　　　　　　　　　　　　pool

　　we lost our bodies in,
　　sound alone
　　survived

Cement sky we were slow to get
going under. Indigent wish for an
   alternate world run out. Flat rock
   skipped on water... The low-lying
                                    sky
      pressed our heads flat, Operation
   Spin, teeth clenched, our heads
   went round and round. I shivered
and shook, finally caught myself,
      hunched-up shoulders no match
                                    for
      the wind, an ill wind we'd heard,
                                    which
      it was... "Lay low lie," we lip-sync'd,
      salaam'd. Peace be with us we
      begged. Operation Kill was afoot,
   we were on the run, ran standing
                                    still,
      paralytic dream come true. Air's
   forfeiture it seemed, we with an
   ear for asthmatic flutes, cement
sky progeny, tribe of late repute,
   beyond only more of the same...

The new day dawned as gray as
   any. Low sky, low ceiling we
stood bent over by, a cold wind
   blew in off the bay... So it
                              was
   and so it went. In cement sky
      country we ate cement soup,
      Operation Grab the law of the
                                    land...
Bread we broke with hammers.
   Crust cut our gums. In cement sky
country we coughed, cleared our
                                    throats...
      Words were at a premium...
      Hemmed and
huffed

•

Planes flew... Bombs fell...
Operation Boast. Operation Lie.
Thug regime scrimmaging thug
    regime, we were in the middle.
                        My
        head was a flat rock the size
    of a silver dollar. The others'
                        all were
    as well... Operation Spin skipped
our heads across water, thin rocks
glancing the face of the water, the
        Dread Lakes eldren were back. A
                                certain
        us, a certain them they related...
    Good's good war against bad they
        were pushing, talking the two
                        again...
    It was Kali's time, flat rocks a
necklace round her neck, heads
crushed flat, slab sky... We were
tramping, trudging, trying to make
    heaven, stuck feet mashing the
                        spot
    we walked circles in, paralytic
        dream's repeat. Ripped ring
    shout, paralytic dream's unend,
                        earth
we receded from... Dwelled on high,
                        low
        sky notwithstanding. No part of it...
Nothing to do with us... Operation
Gloat. Operation Slaughter. Name
after name after name... Not in ours
                        we
        said, slapped heads ringing, not
    to be Andoumboulou again. *Not to
    be Andoumboulou again but were, we
        within we athwart we ad infinitum,*
    voice we were chided by. Bottom
                        voice,

low sky's amanuensis... Low sky, slow
　　start, we staggered, stood our ground...
　　　　Home at last, it said. We laughed...
　　　　　　　　　　　　　　　　　　Jaws
tight, teeth clenched, we circled. Words poured
　　out like sweat... Bullets flew, legs bent,
　　　　　　　　　　　　　　　　　buckled.

　　Square one. Square
　　less than
　one

•

It was the Ricochet Lounge
we ducked into, last call.
Sun Ra played a Toupouri
harvest. "They plan to leave,"
                we
semisaid, semisang, chimed in.
  Hoarse arkestral flutes laid a
rug of water under our feet.
  It was the end of the world
                      again...
A warning song the semisong we
                    sang,
  we all walked circles inside our
heads. Each of our heads an
   aroused ark, a flat rock we
                  rode,
we awoke aboard ship, a spinning
  rock flying saucerlike, obduracy's
day drawn out. Dread auspice's day
a skipping rock we grew wet with,
                    pant
legs and hemlines wrinkling the face
of the bay, at obduracy's behest we
walked on water... Stone ark we
  stepped and stood on, miraculously
flat, spun with, could barely keep our
                    feet...

  Obdurate sky the it we sensed wrote
   epitaphs on, we without world or
it without us, circling square less
than one, centrifugal, farther out
                 the
  longer we walked. Choked up
wearing epic shirts, moot ribbons,
   ythm's day begun... We were
  he's and we were she's, each
one or the other, felt between our
                 legs
divining which. Home where there was

none, stone as close as we got,
talking the twos again... We were
  I and I, each I another, felt among
ourselves fathoming which... One
                                    was
dreaming again, lost to us dreaming,
                                    dream-
  ing us lost
again

•

If I stood I stood in line like
everyone else. A lone pigeon
pea lay on my plate... Growls,
 gruff stomach. Polyphysite
                              cry...
 Hell was holding elections
                              again...
 Breastbone would be our pillow,
Kali flatchested of late. Stuffed
  her bra with the rocks our
heads were, were she to wear a
                              bra...
 We stood in line waiting to skip
  our heads across water. We stood
in line, each awaiting our turn. We
stood in a straight line, an unwound
                              circle,
  our own heads between finger
and thumb as if ours to throw, we
stood on the shore at the bay
skipping stones or we stood on the river
  bank up from the bay skipping
                              stones.
 Water and sky were one I wanted to
say... We stood on the shore at the bay
harvesting rocks or we stood on the
river bank up from the bay harvesting
                              rocks.
 The river ran to the bay... One was
everyone within, all in one I wanted
to say, graced moment gone away from
  again come back again, back but a
                              wisp
  of itself, ghost moment, proof it lay
                              else-
  where,
  prod

SOUND AND SUBSEQUENCE

—"mu" forty-second part—

Next it was Nub's new colony Quag
we were in, music's weapons for the
   weaponless not the ones we were
   looking for. Struck zithers lay in
                           wait
   behind a bush on the side of the
  road, spike fiddles lay in wait as well...
  "What it am," we blurted out without
thinking, throwbacks against our
  will. We were there at B'Head's
                       behest,
   melon patch inhabitants airlifted
in, smashed heads marked our spot.
  We moved in as night fell or as
                     day
  broke, little way of knowing which...
We lay stitched into the landscape,
  dressed in laugh jackets, naked if
                   not
  for scrub we crawled under... We
lay on our stomachs, a flat planet lay
  under us it seemed, cloth our laugh
                     jackets
  were made of made us giggle, giggle part
   wince, wince part giggle, rough threads
  worked our ribs. We lay stitched into
   Quag's interior face down, sniffed
  our jackets' bouquet... Made-up odors
                     made
us giddy, gas we'd have sworn it was,
  scratched-up elbows we pulled our-
  selves along on, legs and bodies dragged
   in back... Moaning voices lay close
  to the ground, an acoustic scrub we
                   inched
  our way under. Lay close, cut upward,
   singing some called it. Keened, kept us
going, kept us at bay... Laughing not to

cry but cried even so. That we were
                                there
but not there was no relief. "Aman, aman,"
    we made out, not sure what we made out,
                                        knew

    not admitting
we knew

•

Come what might've been morning they
opened their eyes assaulted by leaf-light,
sun's bounce of image off topside,
   underside, looked, it seemed, again
up Sophia's dress. The same song
                    we'd
have sung they sang. Buttocks as-if'd
   into his outstretched hand, he the
high priest whose apostles they'd have
  been, aromatic loin-gap's evaporative
adamance,   fruitlike lower lip...
                  What it
  wanted to say left unsaid again, as if
to be was to be always elsewhere. A
room with no fourth wall missing, no
  one outside knowing what went on...
                 Late
  afternoon it turned out to be, the
apocryphal she newly draped in
   sortilege. *This the new goat-faced*
  angel, the would-be book they'd have
                 read
began... So spoke the he they sang of.
So, had there been a book, the book they
thumbed... So said we, translating the
  ground we lay stitched in, sung-about
                sophic
  light we lay deprived of, leaf-lit embroidery
                  lit but

  invisible, song's moot
  suzerainty
crushed

———————————

The motion of tones telling sight's
demise, the motion of tones beaked
and feathered we sensed. We lay so
    still we felt a tree fall a thousand

                                miles

    away. Outside such as it was we
        turned in… Turning into birds we
cracked seeds between our teeth. It
    was the morning after sight's
    demise, we disembarked. A

                        boat
we thought it was we'd been on.

    Goat-faced allure we could only
imagine, a satyr's trunk translated
    upward we thought. A rain of black
hair obsessed over, the tip of his

                                tongue
    assessing her lips, teeth, tongue…
    The same song we'd have sung, leaflit
abscondity. Leaflit revelation, sophic
    rump… Better not to've seen than
        to've seen what we couldn't have,

                                better
        to be blind we'd have sung… Eked-
out accompaniment the world ours
    fell away from, the motion of tones
                                having

        nothing
        to say

―――――――――――

Basking aloft in bodily heaven we
came down. Quag's malaise lay
behind us even so... Sophia sighed,
wanting something else. She
                                        heard
the woman with the bell in her
throat backed by strings, adieu
backed by rattling drums... There
was a man, she said, liked it she let
his hand up her leg, said it so
                                        near
the near side of singing she sang,
song so understated we wept. Sang the
moment living unsung time, she said,
mouth a mere slit, rude amenity, she
                                        said
she wiped spit from her lips after they
kissed... Made-up words the
words they sang, the song not one
they knew, Quag's high country
                                        Sqat
filled with helium... Wind... Warble...
Snort... It was the song, newly
known to us, we'd sing forever,
lost utopic wandering, toetip to
                                        head
of hair

SONG OF THE ANDOUMBOULOU: 64

—sound and sediment—

In the alternate world
another alternate world.
I tore off and I turned
    away. Alma Bridge
                Road
    I turned off on, non-
  allegorical water on my
right, allegorical water on
my left... The left side
    said the soul was
               burnt
    wood. Soul was only
     itself said the right...
Sweet beast in whose
belly we fell asleep again,
               the
     sweet beast music was
    we'd be. I was pinioning
  light's incommensurate
     object. I wanted the
    baby's cry to mean I'd
              begun

  again

       •

Soon it came time to go,
the one thing we'd hear
no end of. Going newly
           sung
   about known from day
             one,
  tread of light newly blue
unbeknown to us... Earth
fell away toward water,
   dreamt or imagined
           incline,
newly anaphylactic walk...

Began to be gone away
from, soon it was a train we
were on. In the club
                              car
toasting time, drinks lifted,
                                        people
getting ready not ready, an
autumn note suddenly
                              struck.

Where we came to next I
    was lately an elder. Spat rum
rode my head. Torn organ
I wanted to be done with, I
                              lay
on my side hearing a baby
                                        cry...
Late moment gotten back but
altered, endlessly not what it
was. Nub was to Quag as
                              he was
    to her, we to what what they
    sang disguised... Goat-
faced abatement might've
    been bird-faced, warble an
                                        acoustic
    feint... Sun streamed in thru
    the leaves, branches, light
                              between
    lubric legs. We were men,
    were it light between a man's
legs women, women, were it
    light between a woman's
                              legs
    men. So light's amendment
                                        went...

        Light streamed in, the air
        suddenly strung, none were we
                                        either,
        both

•

It wasn't light we were
attended by. Dark lay
  under the leaves and we
                            with
  it, we for whom the rain
                        would
come... Not to be known what
  we it was, its or another,
  water, falling star, non-
equinoctial slope gone off
                        of,
  what what it was no longer
was... Had it been a house Quag
  Manor we'd have called it.
No roof bestowed its blessing,
                            no
  walls kept outside out, no way
  could we say it was a house.
    We thought it a gloam state
    scatting its whereabouts,
    tongued runaway, talked out
                        of
our heads... All we knew was
    the two we were divided
    by, pungent book where their
legs met sung about incessantly,
                        said
    to be where ours would end up...

  In an alternate world it was other-
      wise. Dreams wore off and we were
    only as we were, dreamlessness no
                            dream
anymore

DOUBLE STACCATO

for Thaddeus Mosley

A tipsy walk the walk we took.
Tilt had its way, teeter. So to
   say, so to say, we said,
   wood's whatsaid serenade
   emulated, "mu" forty-fourth
                      part...
A closer walk thru the forest of
semblances nicked our skin. Wood's
   near side leaned in, leaned out.
   Gouge's gospel it was we
   brushed against, wood's new
                  kingdom
   come... At blade's edge ground
   gave way. Planetary mend, ad-
   monishment. Legs abruptly
   rubber it seemed... Synaesthetic
   snout, synaesthetic eye-slit.
               Head
   broken off come to a point pointing
   up in back, grain plied say on
   say. Grain said say, laid elsewhere,
               lay
within squint's reach... A wobbly walk
                 thru the
   forest of semblances it was. Sledge-
   headed lean looked out at us... Book
   of blade, alphabet of scuff it turned
               out,
scrape, scour, scuff... Water slid ashore
not far away, wood eventually water,
   walk so long sung about closer
   than we thought. Wood said to be
   source as if to say it was once
             water,
wood already water, grain its giving
   way... Sand lay grain on grain, we
saw each one, said or thought we
            saw.

Wave an oblique writing on wood,
                              ripple,
wave our diluvian book... So to say,
    we said, so to say. What I heard
        was in my head, I said, no one was
    listening, wood's walk talked
    even so... What would wood say we
                                    asked
and we answered... So to say, we said,
    so to say... Dark wood siphoning
    light, we leaned in, dark wood's long
                                    way
    home

SONG OF THE ANDOUMBOULOU: 66

—horn council—

In an obscure bin or in an under-
ground vault they found it, *The
Namoratunga Double Xtet
        Plays for Lovers*, the album
    they'd been dreaming of...
                            They
    the putative twins lay with legs
entwined. Bubble where belly
    met groin... Lithe crotch and
ass-crack beneficent... Loin rut's
                                fleet
        perfume... Asked where they
    were going, he said nothing.
All in the end a banality, he
    lamented, there no sooner
    there than gone. The chorusing
                                horns
        wanted a word with him... A
    game of dare the piano intimated,
    some new Eurydice's beckoning
                                walk...

        Exhausted, fell, breath a benign
    feather, mist an amended air
they'd accrue... Would they get
    where they were going, would
                                where
        they were be there, blood on
    its gums and tongue, same
    question, ground we'd give an
    arm to reach we said... They
                                were
as we were, looked at from a
    distance, we them, we the
    chorusing horns lowed and
    coaxed. Could've been
                            right,

could've been misled, an
eventual king at nipple imprint's
   mercy   lighting the screen in
the room they were in... Could've
   stood, grabbed hands, Jah
                       willing,
  could've again gone off into
  Nudge... Doings of the not yet
                  utopic...
  Eternal return locked in
  apoplectic
light

         •

We the chorusing horns mourned
and amended, looked and but for
   make-believe break saw nothing,
  dubbed it Ass Valley they were
in. We the chorusing horns
              bellowed
   and blew. Namesake noise...
  Nonce prolegomena... Bray
what we named it next... That
  there was music made them
  wince, weary, a reminder it
              wasn't
music they were in... She said
it felt like nothing, touch and
  say love though they did.
  Too bleak, we the chorusing
            horns
admonished, star-spark lighting
the bells we blew thru, we the
  chorusing horns blew an
  answering run... Nothing,
          she
  repeated, caressed his
           cheek
  nonetheless. Anuncio she
called him, whispered it again,

again… Gone in the head, we
    hauled a wagon filled with
                           rocks,
    we the chorusing horns whose
                             will
   would nowhere near
be done

In the one world moving on, in
the other getting back where
    they'd been. In him some-
  thing sunken she caught a
    glimpse of she'd lift out,
                                    ledge
      he lay stranded on... The
    chorusing horns' remote
  counsel, drift it washed up with,
      each its own way pointing
    skyward, Namoratunga stones
                                        each

    aligning a star... Lit pictures
of the on-again war filling the
    screen whose light they lay
                            cast
    up in. The chorusing horns'
      ostensible roar newly
    moot, wave-crack snapping
                                the
    coast

•

Scared. Shivered. Shook. Hard
unheard-of aggregate. Edge
we led them toward... They lay
kissed by seafoam, sand
                          on
their skin, dream they knew
no way not to be dreaming,
    dream they sat caught up
                        in...
They sat on the floor sipping
lukewarm tea. Incense opened
our noses... Spliff-tip chalice
more reed than reed was,
                          we
the wandering horns looked
on. Stood, standing stones
leaning skyward, "Nyabinghi
Swing" the new tune in our
                        book...
They sat cross-legged on
the floor, short of lotus, lay back
between table and couch. In the
upset zone known as not
                        yet
there they reconvened, she
unexpected harmony's ghost,
    another she recondite solace's
regret... They sat on the
                        floor
sipping herb as we looked
                        on,
incense an androgyne funk,
flesh crevice, book of anabatic
recess... Might've been better
had we not been there, better
    to've again been as it had
                        been,
no nonce ensemble breathing
in, breathing out... They sat on
the floor, they began to get

closer, abstract accomplices
Anuncio sat with, one we called
                              Sarah,
   the other Celeste, we saw what of
it we saw in retrospect... On the
decline side of memory they
   survived, waves and cold
   wind outside the room they
                              sat
cross-legged in, known if not
long to've been there, long time
   coming, long time gone... They
sat on the floor, they began to
   get closer. Eventually they
                              climbed
   onto his lap, sat on his lap, they
   swore they'd never been
   so forward before... "Times
turn," we said in so many words
   had we used words, blurted
                              out
   as we looked on. Gruff tongues
                              egged
   us on, wagged in back of us...
   Cupping horns they wanted
us to be... Gravel roughed our
   throats, grievance, grudge,
                              teeth
what stars were before they were
                              stars,
   teeth taken up thru
                    smoke

In an aggregate wind or in an
undeclared war they saw them-
selves. A blow-by interstice
they found themselves in,
strob-lit gust we found ourselves
                              caught
up in, wind an arpeggiated run…

A shooting star it might've been, it
moved parallel to the ground, foraging
horns we turned into. Rummaged
Ass Valley, ghost writ we called
                              it,
groped, made braille each
other's newly open book, they
the aroused we we let loose…
                              We
were the dreamt-of ensemble we
insisted, heard, unheard,
unheard-of, they the idyllic
                              two
we played
for

•

Flat rocks, we lay curled
inward, cats curled sleeping
  it seemed. In love with
    gravity it seemed or we
                said,
    we the chorusing horns
  at large again. Obdurate
    sky we lay low extolling,
                  stone
canopy. Underness, recondite
  remit... Obdurate sky no
  pilgrim's inn, rock pillow.
Scat-sung insinuance weight
                would
    accrue to. Nothing we
    would say sufficed... *Over-*
    stood we wanted to
    say but said nothing,
             word
  on the tips of our tongues
  reconsidered, fix we drew
                 back
  from

·

Next where we were was
known as Tumbling Down,
   ass's earth curvature
   an evaporative gauze,
                           cloth
   an abrupt poof between
fingers and thumb, none
   of us knew what next...
                            No
   longer what we were, we
were athwart what we were,
   exed, exhausted, aroused,
                              elegiac,
   depth all echo it seemed... We
   were intimacy's amen corner,
caroling horns having our
   way with wingdust, hating
   it having to be that way...
                              Late
   Billie's book it was we
took a page from, voice
evacuated, cracks where
   accents fell, bent-key mag-
nanimity rebuffed... Names no
                              end
   and in love with trouble, Back-
   bite Syndicate the name
   we now took, Billie behind
                              us
now. A moon made of glue
   hung above and in back, we
stood in gluelight. Hung by
   a thread, ball of thread,
                           stuck
   surrogacy, rolled as night
wore on... Moon could only
   do so much, we admonished,
long since not as it was or we'd
                              heard

it was, not to be wished on
again... The beat, we admitted,
    was time, took us out, string-along
moon at our backs notwithstanding,
    strumlight wrinkling the backs
                                    of
our necks... Gouge eye, twinkling
                                    tarpit...
    None of us looked in
    or looked
back

———————————————

A nonsonant serenade it must've
been. We blew but no sound came
out… Him and her dreaming
and her dreading him between
                              other
legs, him dreading others between
    hers… A steep wall we were
    even so, leaves curled and
lifted by wind. Curled, burnt,
  brittle. Scorched on their edges,
                              broke.
    Bridge between one world and
    another, bent limbs. Legs, arms,
                              ears

    gently
bent

　　　　No sooner that than we
the chorusing horns revived.
　　Soul stones mounted our
　　　　backs but were mute. None
　　would say what soul was.
　　　　　　　　　　　　　　We
asked. We asked again… None
would say what soul was, ask
　　each one though we did.
　　Soul stones climbed our
　　　　　　　　　　　　backs
　　even so, rode as we stood
　　　　　　　　　　　　stone-
　　like, asking
　　what soul
was

SONG OF THE ANDOUMBOULOU: 66½

Egypt 80 it now was
I was in, stiff reed
stuck to an overt lower
lip, bite what being
                    ready
    was. Electric wires
around my fingers
to make it more
        real, Fela's wide
    awakening the
                    caul
I looked in thru…
                    Umbrage…
    Airegin all but gone…

    Talked off the ledge,
looked out at the sky.
Wanted shadow to
    unwrap light, light
                    shadow,
    should've-been graces
    bestowed at long
    last, stick limbs thicken
        as we trudged… I
    wasn't he of the he
                    and
    she we'd serenaded,
no longer one of the
    chorusing horns as
well. I wanted to say
                    "we"
    but "blocked advance"
                        came
    out, gutstrung box the
sound of a cello bowed
    with a saw,   Quag
suddenly faded from
    view… But it wasn't
                    Quag

we saw fade from view.
  Some called it Qraq,
  some called it Ouab'da…
    Ripped, immemorial
                  kiss
  we chapped our lips
  on, stuck lips cut from
               wood…

  So regardless where I
stood I stood elsewhere,
  counseling horns at
  my back no consolation,
              stuck
    refrain I stood listening
  to. It seemed regardless
where I stood I stood
  legless, shook my head,
    shaken head shaken
              free
  of what fell out. Napped,
immaterial this, that, the
  other… Seedpod… Mother-
in-law's tongue… So if I
  sat I sat in convalescent
  light. Island air, drizzling
             earth,
    grounded, galactic horns
    gouging my back… Regard-
less where I stood everywhere
I stood I stood elsewhere,
    stubborn horns insisting
    I stood elsewhere, staggered
               address
  I stood leaning
  toward

Thompson transforms the stable in Piero's painting into the black, shadowy silhouette of a huge bird, its looming darkness suggesting Thompson's own conflicting use of bird imagery. The orange figure, distinct from the others in color, stands directly behind the kneeling figure of Mary (rather than off to her side, as in Piero's version) and reaches an arm up toward the bird.

—Shamim Momin, "Commentaries,"
Bob Thompson

BLUE ANUNCIA'S BIRD LUTE

after Bob Thompson

Bedless trek she saw
them embarked on. Choked
earth they were strewn
across... Sleepless,
                walked
in their sleep she said it
seemed, yet-to-be world
on the tips of their tongues,
each in the other's
                eyes no
end... Lost endowment,
indigent kin. Lapsed earth
gone after, something they
                saw
she knew they saw... The
lute's neck's gooseneck
                look...
And so said nothing. Cigarette
stuck to a nonchalant lower lip...
No book of dissolving the
                book
said less... Lithe body had at
by one that wasn't there, hers in
                the
his-and-her ghost house, near
water, nose caught by sea smell,
salt, said to've been known before,

moved on, soon to be there
                                again…
    Patch of hair he put his hand
to. Voice eaten at by what names
fell away from, thrall nothing
there gave its due… Roofless,
                                floor-
less umbra. Patch of hair parting
    the dark welcoming heaven.
    Bound legs of a bird she held
                        on
to… Amniotic light in no one's
    eyes if not his. Hand assessing
her leg mounting skyward…
    Wonderment winged but
                        with
    legs held, hard to miss what it
                        meant…
    Hers to be his to be hers ad
infinitum, smoke smudging
                        the
bell of her throat. To what had
    been or might've been her
    thoughts migrated, cloth wall
                        he
pressed his hand against, he of
    the indelicate embrace. Split
                        stem
of a bass played awkwardly, canvas
                        wall he
    reached in
thru

Udhrite curvature, hand roving
haunch, her hand leavening his.
World a reduction, world we
departed, world we blew up
                                in...
Again we were in southern
                                Spain.
We were in London, maybe
Madrid. Another train pulled out,
    exploded, another bus, cab,
    jet, imminent debris... We
                                were
somewhere else, anywhere but
    there, song piped in from
    nowhere we knew the likes
                                of,
music's we the we we'd be...
We were somewhere else
    wanting to be somewhere,
    whatever crease or declivity
    hid revealed it seemed, music's
                                you
    and I the we we'd be... All of
a sudden subatomic it seemed...
See-thru flutes accosted us... We
    were less than bones underneath...
                                The
    one song the songs all wanted in
    on, all inwardness inside out. The
    one song the songs, added or
    not, added up to, song any one song
                                was...
Two Andoumboulou we were yet to
    meet yet we were them. Again we
were in southern Spain. Song was
    a well, rope tossed into it, water
                                we
again coughed up... Did we fall
asleep not knowing we slept we
    lay awake wondering, sand-

paper blanket the bedding we
got, bed some new regret. Wide
                                    awake
   wondering what would console
   us, free not to know where we
   were... Non-allegorical ground it
was we stood on, likewise the house
                            we
   blew up in... Remembered, yet to come
   it might've been. We the posthumous
kin still wondering which... Allegorical we
   laid us out leg to leg, we lay awake,
                                    night
   we lay remembering twice removed...
All being into ourselves exploded, non-
   allegorical house notwithstanding,
   else what anything was no matter
                            what.
   Again we were in southern Spain,
      sipping wine eating tapas in Córdoba,
a bulería ghostwrote our return... Soft
   cloth atop Udhrite breast, belly, rump.
                            Night
      of not knowing not yet let
                      go

_____

The lovers awoke to news of an
explosion, rolled over, dozed off
    again. Feathers floated up from
their tongues as they spoke, *world*
                                and
    room were the same… What it
                            was
        was outside leaned in, world as
        it was as if never to be other-
        wise, in took outside in… Body
    bomb, soul fuse it appeared, long
                                night's
        loss of soul… Leg to leg they lay,
            each the other's increment, the
                                        we
        they'd eventually
                        be

•

What they thought more real than
what was there. They struck poses,
looked off to the side, song backed
by strings in the background, the
                                    word
     feliz came up, kept coming up...
     Day yet to arrive the one
                              song,
  sung loud, whatsought, sunlight
  long since gone. What they thought
  we saw, saw thought, no secret...
Fold and recess gave up all inti-
  mation. Overt. Post-Udhrite...
                              Raw...
Nothing stood still, they were in Cape
                                    Verde,
     the word *feliz* kept coming up... Strings
  took them up to a hilltop they were
children on... They were on Eleuthera,
  the mountaintops of Atlantis... Rag aria.
     Imminent apocalypse. Everything
                                    torn,
     blown up... In a dreamt opera the
  air ignited. Stiffening ripples got to
  them again... They dreamt they fell
asleep during intermission, lay on the
  floor in a back row, felt each other
                                    up,
     awoke with their clothes almost
  off... Hated that being all they could
  do, not what was but what might've
                                    been,
     the awaited blow the blink of an
                              eye
  away

"While we're alive," we kept
repeating, kissed our lips raw,
pendency's late resort. "While
    we're alive," we repeated, oath
we cut short, feathers massaged

                                      our
    throats... Where we were we'd
been before. That we could see
    ourselves meant we were them...
Outside, looked in, looked out
                                   of it.
    Ragged... Bleary... No sleep...

Posthumous glimpse a leaf catching
light an abrupt wonder... "While
    we're alive," we reminded

                                ourselves...
Fell asleep dreaming we were
                            awake
awaiting sleep... Tight-eyed wind on
warm water moved in, storm we'd be
                                inun-
dated
by

_____

    Again we were in southern Spain,
hurt singers coaxing something
   from words we'd left off hearing,
exegetes against our will. Where
                          we
    came to next recalled where
  we'd come from. New Memory
   we named it, we were them
again, we were orbiting an alternate
     sun... Star wobble gave us
                      away,
   big manypointed burst it was
  and we were, ran whatever it
                was,
   ran whether or not we knew
                   what
                         it

  was

DAY AFTER DAY OF THE DEAD

—"mu" forty-eighth part—

"While we're alive," we kept
  repeating. Tongues, throats,
roofs of our mouths bone dry,
    skeletons we'd someday
                    be...
  Panicky masks we wore for
    effect more than effect,
    more real than we'd admit...

No longer wanting to know
  what soul was, happy to
                    see
      shadow, know touch...
  Happy to have sun at our
    backs, way led by shadow,
  happy to have bodies, block
                    light...
Afternoon sun lighting leaf,
    glint of glass, no matter what,
      about to be out of body it
                    seemed...
  Soon to be shadowless we thought,
    said we thought, not to be offguard,
  caught out. Gray morning we
                    meant
      to be done with, requiem so
      sweet we forgot what it lamented,
                              teeth
      turning to sugar, we
  grinned

                    •

  Day after day of the dead we were
    desperate. Dark what the night
  before we saw lit, bones we'd
      eventually be... At day's end a
                    new

tally but there it was, barely
                              begun,
rock the clock tower let go of,
   iridescent headstone, moment's
   rebuff... Soul, we saw, said we
                              saw,
invisible imprint. No one wanted to
                              know
what soul was... Day after day of
   the dead we were deaf, numb to
   what the night before we said moved
                              us,
fey light's coded locale... I fell away,
we momentarily gone, deaf but to
   brass's obsequy, low brass's
   croon begun. I fell away, not fast,
                              floated,
   momentary mention an accord
with the wind, day after day of the dead
   the same as day before day of

the dead... "No surprise," I fell away
   muttering, knew no one would
                              hear,
   not even
me

•

We wore capes under which we
were in sweaters out at the elbow.
Arms on the table, we chewed our
                                    spoons...
      Mouthing the blues, moaned an
abstract truth, kept eating. The
dead's morning-after buffet
someone said it was. Feast of
                              the
unfed said someone else... What
      were we doing there the exegete
kept asking, adamant, uninvited,
                                    morose...

      Elbows in the air like wings, we
        kept eating, rolled our eyes,
                                    kept
        shoveling it in... Day after day
of the dead we were them. We
ate inexhaustibly, ate what wasn't
                                    there,
        dead no longer dying of thirst,
        hung over, turned our noses up
                                    to
      what
      was

It was me, we were it, insensate,
  sugared sweat what what we drank
tasted like. Even so, the tips of
                  our
  tongues tasted nothing, we sipped
  without wincing... We ate cakes,
                      we
ate fingernail soup, a new kind of
  gazpacho, no one willing to say
  what soul was... Knucklebone
soufflé we ate, we ate gristle, eyes
                 we
  took from flies flying backward
  a kind of caviar, none of us wanting
                    to say
  what soul
  was

SONG OF THE ANDOUMBOULOU: 70

for Kamau Brathwaite

Long on strain the song they
were listening to, long on the
story of Balake and Sona,
the Amazons of Guinea were on
                    the box.
    Saw but saw barely looking,
the dead otherwise alive in a
wreath of sound. Saw but saw
  the ghost a close runner-up,
                sound
  so disconsolately wrought...
Another say, a new day of the
dead. Another disc they sat
  listening to lamenting love's
  arrest. Wanted to say we,
              some-
thing said say something else,
  horns infiltrated how they
  thought they felt...   Strewn...
  Stranded...   Scattered...
             Cast
  up wet on some doorstep...
    Knocked, no one came to the
    door...   House of Sand it said
on the mailbox, a place they'd long
  heard about but only heard about,
             rub's
atomistic address... A way the horns
had ravening defeat suffused it all,
  soft glow going if not all the
  way gone, a gourd-rattle shook
    inside her head... Strenuous
             horns
  insinuating no end... Seeds in a
shell inside her head long since
expendable... Rub infiltrated what
             she
  thought they knew best, horns risking

hoarseness, lilt long since absconded
                                                with,
    long since incumbent
    collapse

                        •

    They were in a car when the cut came
on. A world they couldn't reach inside
    the world they were in, a new elsewhere
        rode with them now... They'd been
                                    misled,
        it was a trick, they thought, convinced it
    existed could they find the right
                                angle,
convinced it was there could they go
fast enough, only a passing thought
        it turned out... What was happening
    there joined them, rode with them. Sona
        caught Prospero's eye, they sang,
                                Prospero
    killed Balake... They were depressed, it
was fiesta time. They were trying to be
        festive, more festive than they felt,
        more festive the more depressed
                                they
    felt... Sona killed herself, they sang.
They rode in the rain in a resort town
        south of Lone Coast, coughed up
        dust on a savanna the music mapped,
            asphalt wet though it was...
                                Balake's
        death and Sona's death were on
the box, worlds away but what motored
        them, world they were also in, never not
    somewhere else as well. It was festival
                                    time,
        they were depressed, roused even so,
                                        saw
        themselves more them
        than they
    were

•

I looked in on them listening, hung
back and fell away and talked out of
my head, imagined myself sung
about, the one the guitars disquisited,
                                        the
      one the horns hawed about... Long
      on strain I'd already thought and I
      thought again, announced my new
name Anuncio. Long on wanting
a new plan, a new planet, announced
                                        my
      new name Anuncio, blue Anuncia's
                                        nommo
twin... Late the following night a new view
      loomed ahead, dimly lit house in the
distance... Singalong the wing they rode
on, sound an emolument feet might
                                        avail,
      stepped into the house that wasn't
      there... Another life they might've
      lived came toward them, air scraping
                                        air
      the sound of it, his and her breath
      entwined... Under a table her foot
found his, straught sound heard as
      edict peaked and kept repeating,
                                        nails
on an upstairs floor... They let their eyes
      wander not to be caught looking, house
      full of sound intimating sound's limit,
                                        not
      to be said it would suffice. Rickety
      stilts it stood on stayed up in mind only,
      house no longer lived in looked at, nod
                                        house
      if not new, another
skin

Leaned in, fell back, Anuncio to
Sona's Nunca. Saw them and saw
   myself looking, looked and sang
along under my breath… Sona
                           caught
       Prospero's eye, they sang,
                         Prospero
   killed Balake… Memory it seemed
I heard them sing, misery, words it
   seemed I heard I couldn't have
                       heard…
     A mule's head lay on my chest.
     I smelled its breath. Only when I
                    yelled
    would it
    move

Nod house turned into shout
house. In the shout house memory
said shut up. It said silence,
misery said amen, the mule's
                              head
meant my stubborn lungs...
                              I stood
imagining I fell back dreaming,
    stuck tongue stuck in my jaw
                              broke
    my jaw

In a bin farther back an acoustic
book of the day, book of going
   forth by day... They awoke
  rubbing sleep from their eyes,
                       ready
for the road again... Sweet Nunca
  lay in Anuncio's arms, hand on
her leg his. Tuft of hair his hand
  kept easing toward, Anuncia her name
    again... The house they spun their
                     heads
    in spinning... Spinning bed in the
spinning room they were in... In the
   moving room the world had become
  they kept moving, at last and yet
                  again
    they lay draped in unlay's elegance,
  at last and yet again they lay as one.
In the moving room the world had
  become they moved on, came to the
                city
  of sad children just over the hill they
                  came
   to next... They laughed, not knowing
  where they were. They sat on the sidewalk,
    ticklish, beginning to grow teeth, dressed
  in loud jumpsuits, drunk. They were
now no longer two, more than two,
               glad
    camouflage a mask they wore... Sad
    eldren, eventual mystics, orphans
   they'd eventually be... Soon it all
              got
  quiet, string tapped on by thumb, heel
of hand, hand itself tapped addressing
   abstract integument, boyed and
             girled
  each other no end... So sang the exegete,
  crooned it unconvinced, doubt chorusing,
                "Would

it were so..." They were children again,
illdren, unlay's lone resort...
                                    "Would
would were shed," they'd have
                                    sung
back

                    •

    In a bin farther back *The Double
Xtet Live in Chicago*, the acoustic
book they found word of themselves
in... Something seen in a face
                            each
would have given an arm for,
reach without end even so. Dark
looked into, light looked into, glad
sad animals again... Holes where
                                    the
stars were they fell from, mythic
                                    seven
turned ythmic two... Holes where
the buildings had been they blew
up in, collapse the band said it
                            saw
would come... "Namoratunga
                            Swim"
it might've been, pooled eyelight...
                                    Eyelight's
    involute
    stir

Stared into what wasn't there, endlessly
athwart what was. Receding lake front,
   Lake Turkana. A burial ground it
     might've been... Laughed-at
                    jook,
   laughed-at pirouette. Lower lip
weighted with pendants made of
quartz, fallen, they said, from the
                   sky...
   Dancing rocks the band had been,
                   balletic
 stone. Stone soul said to've said it
   would have none of it, rocks in a
              ring

  or in a
  row

•

Then again they came to the city of
sad children. Sad glad children sat
  on sidewalks, tenement stoops,
  sad glad faces in windows all
               the
  way up... It all sat receding
  bleacherlike, farther away as the
  buildings rose. Tilted buildings,
                  dirty
  windows, a grin inside each one,
  the children not overtly sad, only he
and she were... They were worried
  a bomb would go off, afraid there'd
  be an explosion to make it more
                 real,
  pinched each other wanting to wake
                 up...
  Then again they lay like stones letting
  the horns do their screaming, unlay's
day undone. The acoustic book a book
  of slipping in, slipping out, wind a
               book
  of lipless kisses... "Came to the
  city of sad children" kept echoing,
  riff they cut their teeth on, riff they
               were
  caught up in, sad glad faces arrayed
in rows receding upward, sad celestial
  atrium, sad gladiatorial stra... Every-
  thing they saw some unexpected
  recess turning outside in, everything
               they
  saw they saw going away... Beauty
             nature's
  hook, they said, gnostic hostages, nonce
  ensemble it seemed. The more they
  now were not many the more they
              were,
  they the exiguous two... That
  there'd be more to it they thought,

deeper they thought, unable to flare
their nostrils wide enough. Recondite
                              book
by turns pungent, perfumed, heads it
   made spin spun off at the neck,
   thrown rocks the world had become.

   They breathed in, the book a book
   of breathing in, breathing out,
                                 un-
   able to breathe in deep enough...
                              And so
they ate, unable to taste anything, drank
unable to quench their thirst. Blurred
   outskirts had them wondering what
   it was they'd come upon, "Came to
                                    the
   city of sad children" still echoing,
                                 again
      she rolled over, again got out of bed,
      glimpsed ass again the bloom he reached
   out for, book tucked into itself... "Came
   to the city of sad children" kept echoing,
                                       reprise
      insisting reprise meant something,
                                      mere-
   ness no one would
   touch

·

Sounds melding notwithstanding, no
merging of souls. They were children,
glad sad eldren, beginning to like being
   afraid... They were afraid a bomb
                              would
      go off, afraid an explosion would
      make it more real, afraid only blowing
up was real... The Namoratunga Stra
Nonsemble was now the new name the
                              Double
   Xtet took, x equaled zero. Somewhere
                                 someone
      whispered it was all a charade... A spinoff
band it turned out to be, burred breathing
to cloth accompaniment, "Flown Youth"
   an old release it insisted they hear... Warm
                              air,
      molecular water. An evaporative world each
      bandied about. Each a mere part blown into
                              balloon-
      like, each a remembered whole blown up... In
      the alternate world an alternate outcome... Pinched
                                 each
   other. Felt it. Let
   go

Accordion bellows were lungs they
heard wheezing, asthmatic firmament,
winded ballet. Palpitant flesh, flat rock
    they lay convinced it all was, laughed
                                        at
    ever having been laughed at, unlay's
                                        tilt
    and redress... Boca del Cielo they set
    out for, his and her heavenly mouth.
      Namoratunga's faraway walk they
    walked, walk so far afield of itself
                                        they
        stood, static picked up from the
                                        sky...
        Raspy heaven horns crying like
    children pointed up at, unlay's burlap
                                        canopy,
        unlay's black
        burlap

•

No melding of souls no matter
sound's intimation. They were children,
glad sad eldren, learning to like being
afraid... They were afraid a bomb
                                    would
    explode, afraid blowing up would
    make it more real, afraid only blowing
up was real... The Namoratunga Stra
Nonsemble was now the new name the
                                    Double
    Xtet took, x equaled zero. Somewhere
                                    someone
    said it was all a charade... A spinoff
band it turned out to be, burred breathing
    to cloth accompaniment, "Flown Youth"
        an old release it insisted they hear... Sounds
                                    melded,
        souls nowhere near following suit... They
        pinched each other proving it posed, made-up,
                                    bit
    each other, loath
    to let
go

          —————————————————

    Where they came to next was
  no Boca del Cielo, no mouth lay
  beckoning above. No generous pout,
    no erogenous lipsmear. Unmade
                             faces,
    root, stem, firmament, unmoist kiss
    what kiss there was... The city was
    inner it was easy to say, anywhere
  inwardly elsewhere, they were them-
    selves ahead of themselves... Dry sky,
                            dry
    scrub, dread atrium... Dome looking
                         down,
      fraught brow... Mouth all churchical
      forfeiture, front, city said to be inner all
                             they
  saw

SOUND AND SUSTENANCE

—"mu" fifty-first part—

We stood on a balcony if
not motherless mothered
by morning's retreat, the
   orphans we'd someday
                     be.
Carnival's end came accost-
   ing the rooftops, Quag's
necropolitan skyline a perch it
   seemed we stood on looking
                     out
   from, looking down. We stood
on our perch, feathered arms,
   feathered bodies, feathered legs,
    ribcages birdcage thin... We
                  stood
   on a flagpole, feet clutching the
ball we stood perched on, waving
   the pole we stood on, possessed...

Two-bodied birds it turned out we
    were, Nub's necropolitan outpost
a robot baton we stood on both
     ends of... Two-bodied birds
   dressed in doublebreasted suits
                 it
   turned out, tarbodies underneath...
Where we stood intimated what
soul was... Unsung saeta set to moot
accompaniment... Time tore by
               below...
   We stood on a ledge. We stood
on a plank. Where we stood shook
   the threads of our suits loose. Wind
blew thru skin it seemed... Where
              we
   stood infiltrated curvature, core,
               nothing
   lay deep enough to escape... At our

backs blared echoing brass. Reminiscent
  regard. Upstart regret... Where we
stood impudent reeds kept at us,
                     yester-
  day's news borne by chorusing bells
                          again,
carnival's gone-again
kiss

      •

  Pigeons what we thought were doves
cooing. Shrugged, how were we to
know... Rats with wings, Itamar said,
  we threw rocks at them,   we of the
                      golden
  shoulders, we of the golden elbows, we
of the ecstatic barrage. What had been
brass became guitar clamor, we whose
heads lay elsewhere caught in cross
                  cover,
  "Anouman Sandrofia" was on again...
We were in Abidjan, crossroads kin,
perch turned undulant roadway. Where
we stood was a ridge we strode across,
                  strode
  standing still all the same... Balcony
rail we leaned against, clung or would
cling to, buoyed by background clang,
declamation, sound our lone support, sole
  sustenance, sound our adjutant ghost...
                    It
  wasn't Abidjan we were in but only seemed
                    so,
  sound's insinuation egged us on... Carnival's
end was afoot, ever-after's morning after, long
                     since
not what it once
had been

There we stood leaning forward, one
hand gripping the balcony rail, the
other an Asafo flag... We were on the
                                    Asafo
flag, two-headed eagles holding headless
                                    "rope,"
we were Nub's necropolitan police. We
were on the flag we stood holding, Nub's
new conscripts, mobius the hold we had on
where we were, appliqué figures, cloth...
                                            We
were real it seemed, more than cutout. It
seemed seeming so we were... We were cloth
                                        filled
with flutter, flap, featherless, birds in word
                                        only,
cut from
cloth

•

There we stood looking out at the sky,
lit sky bursting with sparks the night
before, cat's-back sky arching over us,
clawed feet scratching the balcony
                              floor...
Carnival's retreat left us wondering
where we stood, costume courtesy a
thing of the past. Fireworks the night
before kept exploding, more and more
                                   real
the more carnival receded, more and
                                      more
like war the more we stood beset by
vertigo, more and more the more Quag's
                                    ashes
fell... No matter where we stood we stood
exposed. Quag's fallout put our feet to
sleep, we stood on pins. Feathers flew...
Threads unraveled... Itamar's bobbing
head said we were soon to be debris,
                              Nub's
new macoutes, flags notwithstanding, Nub's
                                      new
burlap sacks... We were wishing we were kids
again, ate popcorn, played arcade games, a
day at the amusement park... Lone Coast
boardwalk about to be washed away,
                              we
stood looking out at where Mu had once
                                 been...
No matter where we stood we stood un-
steady. No matter where we stood where
we stood would not stay put. We of the golden
                                       sole,
we of the golden instep, we of the golden ankle
                                        even
   so

The day before the morning after
was all outwardness, what would
otherwise not have been. Golden day gilded
in retrospect, day-after-day's bequest...
                                   Quag's
      new truth, we swallowed look-like,
      birds in reverse disguise... Look-like fed
      us, food for thought, food Quag's
                              ash
            took the taste from. Burnt book of
            glimpse, glance, eyelight... Look some
                                              said
            soul
         was

The instruments faded as the sun
went down. Ever-after's day after
    at last ended. Astral abutment. Cosmic
                                        arrest...
    It was a cappella night at the orphanage,
    carnival's night-after dispatch. Where
we stood felt more and more like arrival.
        Plucked wing feathers fell and were
                                        lifted
        and fell... Night's night-after condolence...
                                        Night's

        never-never
    address

II
QUAG

The Golden Ones move in invisible realms,
wrapt round in our thought as in a mist

—Robert Duncan, *Passages 35*

SONG OF THE ANDOUMBOULOU: 73

      Quag faded or we turned away,
looked away wanting it gone. What we
    were thinking none of us would
say. Quag's ash constricted our
                     throats...
     Even so we dreamt we spoke in
tongues, talked in mind only way
    beyond what anyone knew, no
matter we'd begun to be numb...
Numb notwithstanding, we'd begun
                  to be
    Nub's antennas. We looked away,
     Quag's ash an ultimate lid we saw
things thru, Archie on the box reciting
  "Scag." For all its bareness it gleamed
                 all the
     more, an insistent rub we were caught
    up in, brute koan, acolytes knowing
not knowing, knowing no way our day
    would come... The dead were still in
                 charge
    we saw. Dead reign's thumb... Spoon
in one's eye... Gouged-out epiphany...
                 Quaph...
Premature we called it, exigent, inebriate,
rub we dreamt we shook loose from...
    Post-ecstatic we called it, Quaph we
                called
  it, dreamscape screaming
wake up

     •

I woke up walking, pinched myself, ran,
it was real. Refugees crowded the wharf
    on Lone Coast, came from no one
    could say where... It was raining. The
                                    road
        was wet... Wet, Quag's ash made
        a paste I slipped and slid on, feet no
longer golden, fell... No goal anymore.
No gnosis. No not saying I quit. Flat,
    nose plowing the mud Quag's ash made,
                                    me
            of the once golden chin... It was
            a game, a trick I played on myself,
        snuck back in right away among the
        others, now not only what was left...
                                    Game
over, lapse gone, we were gold again, worked
                                    our
        way out to where the wharf became a
        runway, lift we were caught up in... So it
        seemed and so we said and so it was,
                                    "even
        so" and such a wine we'd have none of,
                                    we
        of the golden tongues
        again

Remorse numbered us among them,
refugees upsetting the boat we'd
heard soul was, ramp we stepped into
it from. We were code, if not code
                              code's
    reluctance, gold eked out as the
    rain would abide, beginning to
    be numb again... We were wondering
    if we were alive enough, wondered
                              how
        much enough was, the enough we
                                    were
        hounded
        by

•

Had we all been beheaded it
  wouldn't have been more
mindless, a bigger mess the
                          mess
    Nub stuck us in. Cement
    sky, cement down to a powder,
  Quag's ash kept coming down.
                          Quag's
    ash kept falling, infinite Pyrrhic
    drift, Lone Coast imbroglio
  beyond what anyone dreamt,
      dream what we knew though
                          we
    did... We wore hoods, we saw
      nothing, blind as could be, heard
  something sung about syrup, lips,
      lemon, east-west melding, qawwali,
                                  cante
    jondo, Seville, Barcelona, Islamabad...

    Broken world it wanted to mend
    bound only in moaning, bond all strain,
                                  all
  stretch

            ———————————————

    Hit on the head, we talked out of
    our heads. Token gold, all hype,
all hustle. Decapitism's day without
  end... We were shipped out, another
                       ship
        one too many. Claim countered
    claim, no letup, claim the closest
    we'd get... We shipped out, shed
skin, back to what billowed, blew,
                     cloth
     atop rattling traps, drum shudder,
                      husk,
     all say-so,
    shuck

LONE COAST ANACRUSIS

—"mu" fifty-third part—

Some new Atlantis known as Lower
Ninth we took leave of next, half the
turtle's back away. Whole bodies
    we saw floating, not only heads...
    Endless letting go, endless looking
                       else-
where, endless turning out to be
otherwise... Woods all around where
    we came to next. We'd been
    eating wind, we'd been drinking
                     wind,
    rumoring someone looked at God eye
to eye... In what seemed a dream but
    we saw wasn't we saw dirt sliding.
    We were back and all the buildings
    were gone. What were cliffs to us
                  we
wondered, blown dust of Bandiagara,
                      what
the eroding precipice we saw... Ground
    acorns ground our teeth now. All but
all gums, we were where the Alone
    lived, came to a clearing lit by light
                  so
    bright we staggered, Nub it was we knew
    we were still in... The mountain of
    the night a mound of nothing, Toulali's
                  burr
what balm there was. Toulali's burr what
    balm, remote though it was, lifetimes
behind us now... Voice laryngitic, lost
    and lost again, blown grit rubbed it
                  away...
Someone had said something came to
mind. Someone had sung something, what
    its words were no one could say. Sang
                  it
    bittersweet, more brusque than bitter,
                  song's

cloth endowment stripped... Choric strain,
repeatedly slipped entablature. Given...
                                    Given
endlessly again... No telling when but
intent on telling, no telling what. Wished
                                    we
were home
again

                    •

Refugees was a word we'd heard,
raw talk of soul insistent, adamant,
    the nonsong we sang or the song
    we nonsang, a word we'd heard we
                                    heard
was us... Wept in our sleep, again
one with what would never again be
    there, raw talk rummaged our book,
                                    the
    backs of our hands written on with
    cornmeal, the awaited ones reluctant
                                    again...
    The city of sad children's outskirts we
were in, woods notwithstanding, woods
    nonetheless, bright light the light we
                                    saw
    as we were jolted, raw talk spiraling
                                    away...
    We were there and somewhere else no
    matter where we were, everywhere more
    than where we were... Where the Alone
lived we donned abalone-shell ornaments,
    light's clarity conceded, night yet to relent,
                                    Toulali
    smoldered on, semisang, semispoke, wrestled
with his tongue it seemed... We trudged in place,
    barely lifted our feet, backbeat hallowing
    every step we took,   moved us albeit we
                                    stayed
    put. We were where we were, somewhere
    else no matter where, evacuees a word we'd
                                    heard...

Stutter step, stuck shuffle, dancelike, Toulali's
croon enticed us, toyed with us, ground gone
                                        under
    where we
stood

Day of the new dead or a new day
of the dead, La Catrina had we been
    farther south... One of us out
of Mexico remembered, with us
                            from
        no one could say when... Day
    of the new dead a new day of the
                            dead...
Wind in off the water blew us there.

    A beat before. Beginning's beginning.
Never to be there again... Beginning beaten
    back, aboriginal. The Alone collecting
                            shells
    on Lone Coast... They were the awaited
                            ones'
        grudge not the awaited ones, the awaited
ones' wish not to be there... Grudge or its
    ghost, grudge against going, grudge to've
    been anywhere at all... Gnostic hostages
                            down
        on all fours, then-again's beginning, beat
                            before
    beginning be-
    grudged

•

We were in the woods again circling,
not far from Lone Coast,   kids again,
wondered why anything was. The city of
sad children a mood swing away,
                                                    we
strode imagining nothing, redwoods
everywhere, muttered barely audibly,
"Nothing is, nothing ever was,"
                                                chill
so intrinsic we shook... No lament was
it, not exactly insight, precocious not
quite what it was. Beginning's beginning
it seemed we came abreast of, beginning's
beginning's ghost... We shivered, would've
                                                            shed
chill's incumbency had we been able,
close but absconded with, all but all
                                                    done,
sperichill we called it, numb... Had
                                                    there
been a song, had someone asked who
sang it,   whitecaps rushing the beach
we'd have said, whitecapped anacrusis we'd
have said, long since there and gone...
                                                        Lower
Ninth had fallen off, protobeat, protobegin-
ning, blow borne before it began borne again,
the one coast it all had become now crumbling,
                                                                world
edge, world rebuff... Circling no end it seemed,
    except we stopped, stood looking at the sunlight
streaming in. Churchical some would've said but
we resisted, felt it that way but wanted not to. Not
                                                                    was
no guarantee... Circling no end it seemed... Same crowded
                                                                        same
crowded same, ad infinitum, beginning's
beginning's
bluff

No Tchoupitoulas. No St. Joseph's.
The Alone's Lower Ninth by default.
When we stopped we stood, picked
                          our
teeth with fishhooks. The Alone lay their
nets out to dry we imagined, nets made of
   nothing, nothingness, the non-thing
                          we
      surmised we not-saw... They lay
      their nets out in the sun at the base of
      the slope the woods were on. We
                          were
      them, they were there again, evacuated
      we that we were... We were slaves or
      possessed by slaves, the Alone the
      indigenous ones... I wanted to break
                          free
         but fell as I took a step, felt my knees
         and hands hit the ground, I got back up,
                          syn-
      apse what there was if anything
      was

_____

Wind in off the water lifted the water.
Body of waves lain with lain away from,
    caught in crawlspace, barely got out.

    Caught in crawlspace, barely got out,
an alternate state the nonstate we were
citizens of... Pyramids to projects the
    hill we were on, drift infiltrated for-
    feiture, frame, image not to be lived

                                            up
        to... Up never again to be one with
                                        itself,
    soul dissipate what soul was, beginning's
                                        begin-
        ning's de-
    cree

Stray nation sworn allegiance to seceded
from... Abalone necklaces we wore around
our necks... There was a trance I was
otherwise in, beside myself, a new, no
longer
blue attunement I drew back from,
another new cut was on the box. Another
cut on the box, another nick, a new notch,
splay
state sung to rescinded as we sang, reprise
we broke
free from
again

Cock's crow . . . is the classic Saramaka setting for the formal transmission of First-Time knowledge. (Cock's crow is the hour or two that precedes dawn, when most villagers are still asleep in their hammocks.) ... The knowledge transmitted at cock's crow is deliberately incomplete, masked by a style that is at once elliptical and obscure. It is a paradoxical but accepted fact that any Saramaka narrative (including those told at cock's crow with the ostensible intent of communicating knowledge) will leave out most of what the teller knows about the incident in question.

—Richard Price, *First-Time: The Historical
Vision of an African American People*

SONG OF THE ANDOUMBOULOU: 75

He who would have been hers
had she only known, no longer
he of whom this could be said.
Turned away St. Sufferhead's
Academy, school whose law he
          said
he was... Blubbery lips emitting
what sounded like babble but
made sense, walked as if walking
on stilts. Tread became tremolo,
heuristic demur, began to be verti-
ginous, began to be giddy, began to
          smear
lips again... Thought piled on thought,
thereby lifted. St. Sufferhead's almanac
began to be cribbed in, book of the
andoumboulouous two they'd soon
become, scribble she'd eventually see...
          So
that never would've been better than
barely, lamp no sooner lit than blown
          out.
A dream of endlessness, what could be said
          to've
just begun, muttered while asleep
letting
go

St. Sufferhead's lay perched atop a cliff
on Lone Coast... Sounds of capoeira
drifted up from the beach below... Taste
of each other's breath on their
tongues, they stood looking, talked
while
asleep even so. They stood elsewhere
looking in, faint refrain, dimming
senses, haunted where they once had
been... They looked in, leaned in, listened
in from farther out. Sweat wet their
necks,
their breath dilated their nostrils, musk
they stood riveted by... St. Sufferhead
himself looked away grinning, laughed
recollecting what had been had barely
been...
Buildings lay exposed, Lone Coast eroded,
world
awash with rain as before. Things had moved on,
nowhere near what might've been, far the eye
they
saw thru
now

Church whose canon she installed him in,
Anuncia's waste and regret... Hut more
than house the house they were in, house
hut's avatar... A dozen doors where there
                                        were
only eleven, St. Sufferhead's pelted by
rain. Not unaware of what some would
say, what some would say they considered
        moot... An out chorus kept insisting let
go, not letting go, tugged at a thread had
                                        come
loose. Nowhere near let go, kept insisting,
        sang the andoumboulouous two long since
undone, kiss broken out on their lips like
a rash, kiss was a clarinet reed. Kiss left a
buzz on their lips, kept insisting... Kissed
                                        inex-
haustibly as if to exhaust kissing. Kissed
                                        kissing
        kiss good-
        bye

      —————————————

     They the two whose tale no one
  knew the whole of, the two we, two
by two, would eventually be, might
    eventually be. A cautionary tale it
                          was,
   we were told, told we'd never know
                            the
    whole
    of it

LONE COAST PERIPLUS

—"mu" fifty-fifth part—

They were mapping what was
yet to be mapped, the one coast
we'd eventually reach. Were they
the same was the question
on everyone's lips, lips kissed
                                        out,
come to no conclusion, maze more
than map we could see... We
talked in low tones feeling our
way. Walls leaned in as if
listening, passageways pressed
                                        what
bit of sky could be seen, time's
tease that it survive itself... White
cloud, blue wish to be done with
it, moment they remembered alive
                                        out-
side memory, voice's blue forfeiture it
                                        seemed...
Blue loomed above the maze we were in.
Only a bit of it could anyone see... We
saw nothing. What bit of blue could
be seen blacked our eyes out. Moles
we might've been the way we let our
                                        heads
drop, blinded by the tunnels we burrowed,
                                        black
horizon what we saw were there something
we saw... We heard Fela sing "Original
Sufferhead," we thought we heard it. "Ori-
ginal Sufferhead" was on the box...
                                        We
heard Amalia sing "Estranha Forma da
                                        Vida,"
felt we heard it. "Estranha Forma da Vida"
was on the box... The box was one's
head, one's head a bumped extravagance,

conjured what it wanted one to hear.
                                        All
contrivance lay wrapped in a paper wad,
all extremity... Original dissepiment. Original
    recompense... Wall what stood between...
    Maze more than map, it was a map even so, a
                                        page
we found ourselves written on, written in, book
of the blind mice we now were. Map or no map, it
    was a map... Rat's-ass endowment, indifference
    no end... Said our say, done with it we thought...
                                        Said
we thought and as we said we thought, scat's blue
    regency the sanctum we arrived at, synaesthetic
talk the talk our fingers lit, a braille book, we
                                        felt
    our way... Map or no map, it was a map,
    labyrinth a word we'd heard and were in,
                                        bumpy
    coast we happened on. Maze more than map, it
    drew the world in, extrorse coast it made involute,
                                        in-
vert realm
it rolled
out

We became a tribe recalling the founding
two. Ducked in thru a door, we ate food
from Reunion, island in an ocean some-
     where, we forgot which, ducked in, not a
                              trace
of them there… We clutched bodies, rubbed
each other's limbs, less in love with skin than
the memory of skin, skin's image, all the
                              more
     extolling skin… Sexed insinuance, nixed
       insistence in retreat… Would-be what-if,
                              what
     if… We wanted it back, big promise, portent,
                              apocalypse,
     urgency, plummet,
                    plunge

•

A cloud of aliases loomed in
front of us. Hit-on-the-Head
  was an alias. Hung-My-
  Head was an alias. Bell-
Rung-in-Heaven yet another,
                        ad
infinitum, Original Sufferhead's
original headache took us in. We
  stood, stayed put but were
                     moving,
  the turning floor the world had
  always been suddenly new, spun
    heads hurt by what light we
    now saw it with, beginning
  to be wise we thought... So it
                was
abideth lay lightly on every tongue.
  It was an olden book we were in.
Original Sufferhead's lapsarian
serenade we were told it was, floodlit
                reach
  than which nothing could be more
  naked, on to the other side and back
              it went...
Afterwards what there'd been brimmed
over. Not as it was, it what of it we made
more of, the more we made of it the it
  we remembered, it what of it we en-
  shrined... Having done so was to
              say
we retreated, out so bad we backed in.
  A mapping recess backed up, lay in
back of, hesitation made what soul was.
              Fractal
  recess nothing more could be done with,
    fractal correction edged or induced...
              Hesi-
  tation finally say what soul was we wished,
whim we concocted, whim we resorted to,

wish we were compromised by... Onset
                                              of
     the always new was what we'd been
        after, now not so much as a thought.
                                        Naked
     promise we stood astounded by loomed and
                                              lay all
        about, loomed and lay
        wounded, laid
     waste

Island in an ocean somewhere not
only an island in an ocean somewhere.
    Reunion we were quick to decode.
    Wished-for remedy, dreamt-of
                                return,
awake less alive than asleep it seemed
of late, each the other's dream had only
                            dreaming...
    "La Humanidad" was on the box, Angel
Canales. A play put on in ribcage theater
unrehearsed. Post-andoumboulouous, post-
amanuensis, rest we were yet to accrue...
                                    A
    double umbrella lay on the floor by the
fireplace, proof that they'd been there,
    the premature two whose brood we
were. Birdgirl, birdboy, ipsic, unexpelled,
                                there
    that we were there that they were there
    unextricated,   there that we be otherwise,
                                    world
    remit

•

It was getting to be their time
they thought. It'd been getting
to be their time from day one, less
   than one. Looked at inside
                 out,
the ins and outs of what it was
they were in less in than out, the
book become a book of abandon,
                     what
   they wanted to say without script
   or intent… A book of being there
   it would've been, would-be book,
crease, crevasse, word all indentation.
                     Inti-
mated woods what had once been a
garden, leaves what had been V's
where their legs met, hair's hint of
   wilderness raw but fed looking,
                  food,
   fed looking beyond… Mussed
                hair's
   invitation. Intimate crux, caress…
   Not that it was that way except
   to say it made it that way, hair's
hint of recondite benefice, life aside
               from
life what soul was… There was a singer
                 singing
fado lamented a certain her, she his pale flame
   whose bloodless look her hair set off,
   hair, he sang, black as a crow's wing.

   They bit their tongues in their sleep,
   it was real, they woke up, talked while
               falling
   apart, made light of it, nothing much else
                 to be
  done

Hold my hand, he said, and she
held it, small amenity they'd soon
pull away from, hedge against
what was to come... The lovers
                                     lay
    unconvinced, fall away forever
the fate they lay subject to, soul
of late a boat body would be no
    berth for, bottomless the room
                                 they
    were in... His body a boat whose
harbor hers no longer was, hers
   whose harbor his had never been,
  at large in the forest they'd been
     in between their legs, woods their
                              reaching
  thru withstood, saw no end, woods their
                                  rough
    limbs gave
inklings of

A new name remembering
   thirteen dead was on the box.
One of seven sets of twins to
   survive. Twins Seven Seven,
                        "Iré"…
   It was day after day of the
   dead again. We lifted shot
glasses filled with salmon fat.
   "No life long enough," we
                   winced.
   We'd been eating tacos and
   falafels filled with confetti,
     shredded newspapers. Head-
lines blackened our teeth… It
                was
   day after day of the dead again.
   Repetition was what we had
and we worked it, Quag's toll
    rose each day. There was the
   it, then there was the it of it,
               less
   itself than a hum even we could
                 see,
Quag Nub's Pyrrhic limb… Some-
one's face was in a window squinting,
   scrunched up, looked out intimating
   what soul was. A bubble in my groin
                  made
me grimace, I looked up, long since in-
sistent we were it, it was us, Osiris's
   chthonic run… Day after day of the
   dead again. Day after day went by
    without emolument. Nub's low
              growl
   and regret… It wasn't run what we
   did, hesitation was what we had, no
step not taken back. Trepidation was
               what
we had. No way could we breathe deep
   enough, brace against what would

come... If we ran it ran with us. No way
could we be alive enough. Bumped
earth escaped us, lost in low scrub,
                                the it
of it given up, let go... There would be
bits of it ever after, its it scattered. This
would be known as time. So we read in
what would be our book should there be a
                                book,
address not arrived as yet, book in abeyance,
book meant beginning to be gone... It
wasn't my face we saw in the window albeit
                                tunes
from my youth were in the book. "Little
Sunflower," "Equinox," "Doxy," on and
on, played by a beginners band. It was a sad
glad children's orchestra, an all-souls band
                                we
were told... Mock-awkward Monk it might've
                                been,
unintended, so tenuous it made us weep... We
sipped salmon fat, beginners against our will.
Vicarious consort, vicarious kin... Washed
ashore no one could say where, mystic
                                habitat,
Quag's necropolitan outskirts, Quaph... Day
after day went by, mock promise. Erstwhile
body, yet-to-be book, box yet to be within
earshot... More ghost of what it was than
an echo, long since not even a shell. So we
                                said
or said we saw, were told we saw... Whatsaid
savvy, apocryphal witness. Long since no longer
its it, more say than saw... Said we saw an
edge in front of us... The way the ground fell away
                                spoke
loudly. A pregnant star, dilated light... It was
the end of something risen, lifted up only to subside,
                                ythm's
hushed insistence it seemed... So it was in what
                                was
always aftermath, day after day of the dead

again, again no longer the it of it it was...
                                        Book
said to be wet with lipsmear, seal against what
                                    was
    to come. Love's chronic lovers Nubstruck...
                                    Quag's
    quaint romance blown up... An ailing voice
    would come out of it, box as much as book,
        sing its heart out we'd say,   begin
                                with
    humming, not the hum from before, Nub's
    alibi, summon something said out of hearing,
                                        mum
amen

LULLABY IN LAGOS

—"mu" fifty-seventh part—

We were above Lagos before
we knew it. Roofless buildings
looked up expecting tips. It was
    lay not low I thought as we
descended. Sprawl crowded
                the
eye as we looked out the airplane
    windows, lay ghost and holy, caught
    as catch could, etch no architect
                had
seen fit... We'd been there before
we got there, unlay's day was back.
    Weak legs lifted heavy feet, we were
    exhausted... Horns were drooping
                lilies
had the horns we heard been there. No
                horns
    readied our way... It wasn't Airegin
    we were in, it wasn't backwards, ana-
    grammic. Sonny was nowhere to be
              found...

Music's where had evaded us, elsewhere's
elsewhere. It still wasn't music we were
    in... It wasn't rightside left, it wasn't
upside down. Fela was nowhere to
              be
found... Somewhere else's elsewhere
attended us. *I dug a hole in the sand*, it
              said,
    I buried my thoughts. Next I jumped
    in, it said, *so no one else would suffer...*
So spoke St. Sufferhead, St. Sufferhead's
    bulería. Again we were in southern
              Spain.
    The it of it its moving on, its noncoinci-
dence, the it of it had hold of us again...
    Not since two sevens met had we been

so fretful. Lejos we thought we heard, we
          mis-
heard lejos. Again we were in southern
        Spain…
 Lagos lay ahead, Spain faded, came up
short, back not being there from the start…
 It wasn't lay, it wasn't low, it wasn't lie,
         we
were lejos. Not that we were there, we'd
 be there soon, we'd be there later, more
         than
 we'd been before… Neither lay nor low,
we heard it said, blow ghost. Soul
 what we rode, we heard it said, blow
ghost, soul to be about to explode…
        We
walked on ball joints beginning to go flat.
We dreamt a dream we kept dreaming, the
 one that would make it right, knew it
 was all smoke but embraced it, onliness's
         wish
well met… We sat at the table that had been
 set for us, gave eating a new name, drank
with the thirst of the dead, called eating
        "chop."

 There was no doubt we were there. The
  way it was and the way we thought of it
  met. The lay ghost went away… Not the
say or the sign but the it of it again, like but
         unlike
 before. The lay ghost no longer stalked us
 we thought, "mu" as in mouth again…
 Roasted peanuts bordered on burnt.
 "Ebolachi" rolled off every tongue…
        It
was "mu" as in "mu" again, not as if but
        the
 is of it, loud Atlantic stretch, Yemaya's
 arch embrace… We bit kola nut, pursed
 our lips, loss the astringent whose taste
        we

had a taste for. Kola nut was all there was
   left... Nub's hand was in the till, Quag's
                                          hand.
      Oil flowed away, flew north... The lay
   ghost hounded us. Place wasn't space
      enough. Spirit flew thru the cracks...
Lay was to low as low was to lie. Unlay
   banked itself... Thought's lag behind
                                       arrival
      resounded. What we said's lag answered
      not in kind but parallactic, the is of its it
an exact, empathic scat, "mu" as in "mu"
   again... Fires light-years away leaned in.
      Traffic piled up out of earshot. Up
                                          and
      down stairs we went... Ritual was all we
                                          had,
      iterativity's it the it of it. We sat sipping
   beer, the is of it a was of it, lay suddenly
      washed away... We were there but not
      there, not exactly nowhere...   Guitar
                                       ping
      resounded for days... Guitar ping rang
   and regaled us. Inside each wave there
      was another wave... One wave rocked
      us to sleep, the other roused us. Unlay's
      proximity exed or annexed us. No doubt,
                                          barely
         begun, we were there...   The awaited
      blow arrived, Yemaya's warning. A rogue
                                          wave
   pushed us farther in... Gristle intimated
      eternity, we chewed gristle, happy to have
                                          sur-
   vived the
   night

Mythology is inevitable, it is natural, it is an inherent necessity of language ... it is, in fact, the dark shadow which language throws on thought, and which can never disappear till language becomes altogether commensurate with thought, which it never will.

—Max Müller, *Introduction to the Science of Religion*

SONG OF THE ANDOUMBOULOU: 79

What there was's jump,
  what could be said's long
   shadow. A story the story
bit its lip on... It wasn't
              that
  what there was was
  what could be thought,
wasn't what could be thought
  was what would be said...
              Thought
was what there was's fallback,
  say, so we thought, the same...

  It wasn't religion we were
              feeling,
  we were lay. Unlay's day had
come and gone... What we felt
  could've been said to be myth
   but we said ythm, first would
   be last we thought... Science we'd
            have
said were it not say's way not to know
            unlay,
  nonce non-embrace lay stood in whose
  way... Lean of limb we'd have been
could we be said to've had limbs, abstract
  intaglio the press of spun straw, soul's
            insatiety
   we'd have
   said

•

Rain met us where we came to
next, mist more than rain. Light
    ricocheted inside it... Infinite
    crystal it would've been were it
                            not
        for blur, had blur not befriended
                                    us.
    Time-lapse amalgam we intuited more
    than saw, ythmic onset or address...

Coastal fog we were told would catch
fire, no matter we'd gone far from
    Lone Coast. Blur so benign where
                            we
        were was known as Prospect, mist
        we heard it said the sun would
        explode... Coast had come to be
            code for orbit, fog planetary debris.
                                    Cosmic
            shade it all got, gathered. Lay followed
                                        lie
        followed low followed lay, unlay's tonic
        dispatch... We were thinking what could
    be said, wondering what could be thought,
        lag snapped its tail in-between... Sibling
        spin, what could be said not only what we
                                            saw,
        blanket of stars farther
                    out

•

No sooner did we think than what
we thought faded, wordless what we
    thought we saw... A new member
                            known
        as Huff joined our group. Strange
        Brother he was known as by some...
        Wind gust his game his name
                        told

us, branch blown off, broken bough...

                              Huff
       pointed into the blur, claimed he'd
       come from it, only blew smoke we
                              thought...
         Blur blessed us it seemed. No way
    could we make out one another, one
    thing from another. We were back
         before we were, back before
         anything was... Blur was all
                              there
         was, nothing was... Huff got into
    our heads, blur made us blink, soul
         a certain bareness we thought... We
         were back to before soul sought
    body, ass-cleft and curvature yet
                              to
    entice, Huff made it seem that way...

       In Huff's domain we saw waves
       come in, swells an emotional debit,
                              light's
         dilated slide... Symphonic sway,
         more feeling than any of us could've
         said we felt... "In Huff's domain"
                              curled
       around one's ear, caught
       on one's
    ear

•

Huff wore wingtips, argyle socks.
He had a way of dancing standing
still. Cushion-footed, cloud-footed,
   postured, posed, moved only
                   ever
so much... Breath up ahead or
in back of us. Were we dead or
   yet to be born we couldn't say...
     Blur but bound inveiglement, blur
                   before
   anything was. Huff had a way of
having it both ways... It wasn't that
Huff had wings on his feet. Wingtips
were a type of shoe. Huff's way had
   it both ways and we were breathless,
                  Huff,
we wanted to say, took our breath away...
Not without breath we'd have been had
   we said it, say's way would have it
                both
ways... Anabatic scat was what it
  was, the underside rising, soon-
come counsel of souls in absentia,
               no
known auspice
left

As a child his first words had been
  "other side," some inkling even
then he'd come from elsewhere, in-
    sistent even then he'd eventually
                       return...
  Mist on one side, mist on the other,
  a thin line in-between. Mist on either
    side, a misty line between, sight
                  bled,
blur ran thru it all... That there was a
  book we'd eventually be in. Yes,
we knew, we'd heard it before, we
    nodded our heads. Yes, we said, we
                knew
  it would come... Huff had something to
                  say, too
  much to say, went on about it,
  wouldn't
let go

In the upper stacks one found a
book entitled *My Friend Huff*. In
the lower precinct the upper stacks
   lay adjacent to, not to be confused
                            with
   lipsmear but was, blur the apostates
misconstrued… "Strange Brother's
   bequest," one heard them whispering,
                            fraught
   lips not to be believed misleading them,
   wish pervading drapes, carpets, dust…

Blur blended with lamplight, dust
   motes opening the book let loose,
                       motes
   the open book
   drew back
from

SOUND AND SEVERANCE

—"mu" fifty-ninth part—

    Suddenly two, they sat side by
side. He and he looked out the
    nod house door... They wanted
      to go back, wanted not to
                  know
    what they knew, looked out at
      the receding world, eyes whiting
over, in dreams repeatedly bid
    goodbye... Choric escort...
                      Chronic
    dispatch... Wondered what but
andoumboulououousness awaited
    them. They were waiting to be
    born it seemed... It wasn't one
                  was
    it, one wasn't enough, he nor he
      the I and I's he and he of it,
    he nor he the he and he's I and
                  I...
Gnostic imposter each according
to the other. Falsetto. Birdbone flute.
    About to be born or about to be
    bodiless, flew, soon to find out
                  which...
Featherless wren said to be what
    soul was, wren if not robin, picked
on, plucked, he number one's en-
    dangerment, risk he number two
    now took... Saw one's other self it
                  seemed
    or at least one said so, he number one
he number two no end... A hole at
    whose edge one stood, looking in,
unspun incumbency's engine, the mo-
ment, what there was of it, all there
                  was...
    But if both neither he the he of it. "Time's
tongue," he said, meaning to say, "Time

tough." Bad leg pulsing with pain at
the hip, he and he the quintessential he...
Time's
tongue was a scroll he unrolled and wrote
on. *Beaked we'd be we read and*
were, book blown open by wind, he
wrote, *winged we'd be, bereft...* He
and
he read out loud in unison, a net of X's
each
annulling the next... Looked out the nod
house, looked into each face. *We'd see*
what face was only front for, he wrote...
Saw
from before, early in life, an earlier life,
eyes looking to see beyond sight...
What lay beyond, intimated by look,
what lay behind, look's far side soon
come... *We'd be beside ourselves*, he
wrote,
a succession of X's. Rapt ecstatics, we'd
see ourselves outside... Faces wherever
he and he looked, each an invitation, soul
a certain bareness he and he thought... He
who wrote was less a he than a committee,
he and
he's X's' I and I. Time's tongue a rough rug,
part brush, part papyrus...Water crept under
the door... He and he sat side by side
braving the nod house. What was to come
all but already there... Quizzical hedge if
not
would-be trump if not nothing... Nothing.
None-
theless
near

The book bit its tail and became a
disc. Spun sonance he and he were
the proof of. What was to come lay
caught between planks... The
floor
torn loose or begun to be, he and
he sat looking out the nod house
door... He and he knew nothing
if not unlikeliness, scrounged amenity
what
was left were not everything lost.
Antiphonal spin toward what tore
loose,
prolegomena, epilogue and prologue
both,
prologue
both

The book as it turned acoustic became
a disc, *The Namoratunga Nextet*
Live at the Nod House, he and he's
eyes were in the sky... Forehead
                              scoured
by starlight... Cheekmeat scuffed by
   meteoric scree... Face wanting to
   be what soul was... He and he's
eyes were rocks outside their
                              sockets,
   lids blown shut by inclement wind,
                                       cosmic
      acidity,
      drift

SONG OF THE ANDOUMBOULOU: 81

for Joseph Donahue

Quag had moved on and we moved
with it, Huff wearing deerskin boots,
  blue deerskin boots, Huff moving
with us we knew. Once there we
                                    sat
circling the fire, glass fire singeing
  the ends of our hair, flames we
backed away from… Someone
    had been killed we saw. That
  we saw was all we saw… Image
                                    once
  thought to be soul stripped of soul,
soul's loss it was we saw. Someone
had been killed we heard more than
    saw, someone shot in the chest
  and the neck… There was an eye
                                    that
  wasn't ours but a made one, glass
cracked up to be more than it was, lens
    was all we saw… Again we camped
on Quag's ragged outskirts, Quag
                                    behind
  glass but in flames,   heat we drew
back from. "There's a me that isn't
  me that looks," we each explained,
                                    all
  of us talking at once. Inflamed by
an image or the wish to be an image,
    it before the it of it all but lost…
                                    What
  look sought to see was anyone's
                                    guess,
    nobody knew,   captious, autistic,
                                    it for
    the it of it,   ipsic,
  itious,
craw

                ●

Soon we camped on the far side
of So That, an edged expanse we
    found ourselves backed up on.
                                    Again
our sense was we were setting
                                out...
Asymptotic the place we came to,
astigmatic. Looking was what we
saw... Odd clime and country the
    least of it, numb light's wide
                                    eye
dumb with what opened it, no
way could we convey what we saw.
Whatsaid apostrophe... What-
    said encumbrance... What was
    but wasn't there... Inconsequential
                                    claim
        named arrival... Infinitesimal
                                    knot...
What look sought to see was cap-
ture, stare's would-be ascendancy,
    blink's plenary star, eyes whited
                                    out
    even so. We were casting nets,
catching nothing but wish, if the
    intransigent it of it, what would be
not what was to come... A siren's
                                    high
cry shook the nod house. No cause
for alarm, we thought. Which is to
    say we were adrift in the tone
    world. No wish but to be one with
    it, no way could we be one with
                                    it,
look's animal insistence held us at
                                    bay...
No less than God's glance was what
                                    look
    was after... Sunset's chemical blush
    peeped in as our tent flap flapped in
                                    the
    wind

•

Eyes all white, rolled back, we turned
in. Look rolled back on itself... Fret
   not, it said, seemed it said, time's
   tongue an intimate river we pitched
                                                  our
   tents beside, furtherance now the
   light look saw beyond. What had
been what was to come look sought to
see again, prospect bound in mouth
                                               pout,
eye sleight, comeliness's day again
   begun... Frail, faint, it signified raw-
   ness, nothing worn under the clothes
                                             one
wore, the underworld underneath... Inside
   our tents glass fires made silhouettes
   look saw from outside, blacked-in
                                      bodies
   look saw were what soul was, pure
                                       delinea-
   tion,   fill, sheer
   dispatch

●

Someone-had-been-shot buzzed in
the background, sight suddenly
  sound, look's late demise.
  Cleft entanglement, angles,
                                optics.
  Blocked. Charismatic demur...

  Might life live down to an image,
  might light reprimand itself,
Anuncio lay back rearisen, stiff
                                member
  standing Osirislike, as if again
to say what soul had been... Strict
  esoteric someone. Stripped
    exoteric sough. None would follow
suit, Huff insisted. Someone, even so,
                                had
  been shot... Glass bubble. Bird. Beaked
                                its way
way outside... Erstwhile ship inside a
                                bottle...
  Soulboat...
                Sunken...
Soaked

                     Coplas
   que nos han matao… Scrolled
    inscription inside the lightbox,
 sound more than light. Winter
                   skin
out for sudden sun scratched and
   written on, brisk wind ravening
                  sight…
   Something seen in a face more than
face made real, blank but for its other
 side… And so it was gone we were
   shown and said we saw, glass
               lips
  announcing it consonant by con-
   sonant, vowel advancing vowel, glass
regress… Something seen, said
   something's exit, there but for
               what
  we saw, said we saw, unable to say
             what
   we saw… Something seen, said
  to be what soul was, dead before
   we arrived or as we got there… No
             one
  would tell us
  which

Coplas, the wind intimated, que nos han
matao. A long song of wandering it was
were it close to song, a long song
of all-but-exactly-there... Lit landscape,
                                    terra
      lucida, caught inside a TV screen...
      Reaching to get inside it, grabbed
ourselves fingerless, pawed at the glass
   no end... Boughs outside our tents
                              bent
      back and let arrows fly... Glimpse,
                              glitter,
      gleam did
   us in

GHOST OF A TRANCE

—"mu" sixty-first part—

Gray morning, blue morning, a
feather blown between. Mashed
earth incumbent, gone up from,
                                    never
   more naked if ever to be naked,
    brink what it was to be on...
Where next we came stick-figure
people greeted us. Abstract
                                    was
abstract, also something else. Line,
   shape, extension each other
than itself, of number we'd have
   said the same... Aspect arrested
us, riveted we stood... Stick-
figure epiphany held us in our
                                    tracks,
   everyone's bones in full view...
                                    Gray
   morning, blue morning, an unheard
string between. Bad heads' morning
reluctance, ennui's next-day dispatch...
                                    We
   were chill, shiver, exegetic sweat, backed-
   up interpreters put upon by sluff, none
of us could say what was what. Pale
admonishment poised upon lack,
                                    like
   to unlike, pale strain recumbent, re-
   combinant, rude amniotic straw...
Took leave, leave long since taken,
                                    awoke
   to what would otherwise not have been.
We contested birth, we wanted to be pre-
andoumboulouous, done-dead gnostics
                                    again...
   Sound bubbled up, it kept bubbling, sonic
   residue, sonic remit. A fickle sonance,
fraught sonance, warning we knew nothing,

stick-figure entourage otherwise issue-
less, beginning to be remiss it seemed...
                                        Erst-
while ecstatics' lapsed enchantment, trance
    gone none could say since when...
                              Ghost
    of what lifted us, ghost what lifted us,
                                  erstwhile
    enchantment between... Fell back, full-out
    extended. Pilgrim someone called me, I said
    no, then I said yes... Brax was on the box
was what it was, toned uncertainty. Stick-figure
    counsel all air, edge, angle, down from where
                                        we'd
    been and we were again where the Alone lived,
        adage, had it not been so abstract, it might've
        been... Long day of the abalone-shell sunset...
                                            Stood
        among redwoods expecting the worst... What
        was of note and what abjured nothing. What
                                            was
    all, none, one, all the
    same

It was the ghost of a trance. I was a
guest of the trance. What went on we
blamed on the ghost… It was the
ghost of a trance, each of us a

                      guest
of the trance. No two times were the

                        same…
When we hit a wrong note we said
nothing. When we hit the right note
we said so what… Tell my horse,
we were told, fluke solace, horse

                    we
were mounted by… What was done
was done by the ghost, gray morning,

                      blue
morning, eternity be-
tween

Told my horse we would gather at
Nod House, down drinks at the
no-host bar. Dirt was in the drinks
                                    we
drank, planet sludge. Double-take
told its horse whoa, told it unwhoa,
back and forth and back without
        end... Talk spun our heads,
                                    told
our horses ride on. Unresolved
which to insist on, stick with. Could it
    whoa unwhoa's ramble unresolved...

    Spinning heads made us feel we sat on
                                        swivel
    seats... Double-take talked us in,
                                    took
    us in

_____

Sat again at the same table, no two
   times the same, twinship long since
gone. Leaned back, the back legs of
our chairs broke, Nod House Nub's

                              new
address... A straining look made our
   faces look raw, made our skin flush...
Dreamt each other's dream, donned

                              each
   other's costume, hosted one another,

                                   one
   stepped in as
   one stepped
   out

The two who'd lain leg on leg
were again with us, whispering
somewhere deep inside each
    of us incessantly, hoist we
                            rode,
    knowing or not… Loss a low
        murmur no one could be rid
of, skin some new announcement
                            again…
    Anuncia fell again into Anuncio's
arms, Nunca's nest, cropped hair
    grazing his chin, his chest,
                            hand
    roving the top of his thigh. What
                            there
    was and what eventually would be,
both pure lipped insistence it seemed,
    lips talismanic it seemed… They
                            were
    caroling love, love's face averted,
    finessing love's hooded look.
Each a recess it stared out from, halo
in back or about, cave-dark areole
                            auric
    it seemed, cave-dark auric of late…

    A thread of woven voices cloaked us.
    We knew we were no longer them.
Spun heads blessed us, a kiss we drew
    back from, bolt upright in the bed
                            the
    new beginning was, no new beginning
                            again…
        It was tell-my-hoist if not tell-my-horse.
        Heist had to do with it as well… We
        stole away, bedouin love more bane than
                            blessing,
    want's want to be done
    with itself

•

Stick-figure greeting notwithstanding,
we moved on, sticks filled in, fleshed
out. It was the city of sad children we again
came to, a point on a circle there was no

                      exit
from, Nunca's new bed or behest not
what we opted for, vestige, aliquant regress...
Reborn we said they were and so it was,
a young mother's toxic milk no longer

                    toxic,
a son's rage laid to rest... Emblem,
example, both ad infinitum, each of
them a tale told again... They sat on

                  stoops
looking out at the twilight, spun heads'
colloquy a congress of sorts, eldren they'd
eventually be... They sat on stoops looking
out at us, moist eyes revenant, moot counsel

                        caroling
no known auspice, phatic or prophetic,

                  mem-
ory's
rout

His and her intimated skin mere tabula
rasa, sneaked ahead and saw what was
to come. They were beginning to lament
    light's arrival, sun some annulment,
                                    day's
    discontent, skindeep endearment snuffed...
Their naked backs were dawn's light
    rescinded, stubborn wish, night without
end... Day gotten up in rags, no regalia,
    wondered what more to do but witness,
                                        witness
    nowhere near enough... Rose divided hav-
    ing lain as one, light insisted, having so
lain a lie, light said, world ripe unrepair...
                                        Rose
    divided multiplied, it said or insinuated, sad
                                        glad
    children
again

Orphans they saw themselves to be...
　　Tight-breasted, large-hipped Anuncia
blossoming downward, Anuncio's com-
pacted groin... Cold brook, white birch
　　　　　　　　　　　　　　　　bark,
　　nod was all outdoors. Land law, land
　　of unlaw... A newborn's cry cried
abandonment. Meth umbilicus. Mother-
　　less one... Ready, they thought,

　　　　　　　　　　　　　　to
　　be done with it, life less itself than
an image, words' rescue, suspect-
　　idyllic might it be said to be idyllic,

　　　　　　　　　　　　　　ersatz-
idyllic if
at all

．

The tale of the two undone
again. A tale of too many,
   the we they'd otherwise
   be, tribe long thought to
            be
lost rediscovered, distracted
   though they were we were
                them...
Slapped heads held a lesson we
were loath to let go. Lived a lie,
   we said reviving it, said but
   unsure of it, cimbalom sonority
                dogged
our feet... Struck sounded like
   plucked, we were in Budapest.
Cimbalom sounded like tendons,
drawn ligament, tight legs bound
                our
   feet. Mihály's horn made us its
   envoy, Trane in Transylvania,
                "Árgyélus"
   was on the box... Lived-a-lie
   was dreamed-a-dream's dark
                twin...
Dreaded moving on, dreamed a
dream of moving on, day's dis-
   content come on by night, bedouin
   ambush, breathed in grieving,
                grieved
   breathing in, drifted farther north,
   fell in the sea... Dreamed a dream
   combing Sedna's hair, grew finger-
less, glad sad ensemble, harps had
                at by
stubs, world we were older in unspun...
   It was an undersea railroad, planks
on the ocean floor, plucked rungs run-
   ning not running up, not running
                down,
   thrummed on-its-way-ness, thump.
                All

thought was in each thrum, all uncertain-
ty, thrumlock knotted, let go… All
Anuncia wanted was to feel fingers
                                          again,
hand clasping hand, only what Anuncio
wanted… Anuncio wanted what Anuncia
wanted: finger find finger, hand untangle
                                          hair,
flesh clothe bone again… It was another
Anuncio, Anuncio the Elder, this had to
do with, a new Anuncio tale our tribe now
told. A wandering band finding our way,
                                          we
spoke of weight, weakening back, Anuncio's
latter-day Legba, Sedna, our lexicon whatever
                                          came
up… Lost amenities led us elsewhere, the every-
where we pretended to be, an everywhere
we all but were and would arrive at, stooped
                                          over
starting over again… A powdered wall we put
an ear to pressed us. What we heard we heard
as if at a distance, far off yet a wall encasing us,
                                          a wall
of powder we put an ear to, custom fit… Somewhere
someone said someone's uncle said something.
                                          Fuzz…
Static… Sunspots… Powdery wall one's ear, curled up,
                                          lay
packed
inside

．

Nod, Huff insisted, nobody home,
windows and walls all smoke. It was nod
as in given the nod, blank check, green
                              light
    given B'Headless, nod as in nodded
    out... Gray day of again going
forth. Metaphoric boat, metaphoric
  embarkation, weakening arms, trunk,
                           legs
      no metaphor... Ribcage intaglio fell
                       behind
    us, body all but all complaint, we behind it,
  a circle of gaps we were on. Valedictory it
    seemed albeit muscular, brass behind it big
as dawn... But come dawn day seemed impos-
sible, Quag's imponderable ash coming down,
                              rain
    we were abraded by... Thrum was back, we were
                            thrum's
    yet-to-be, thrum's intended. Again we lay flat but
                             were
  lifted, thrum's doorstep
  crossed
out

They the would-be we, would-be
founding romance. Would-be *Anunciad*
again struck dumb, music by default.
No high sky… Deep sea thrum…

Mihály piped underwater. Ai Glatson
met Ayler there as well… Chorusing
horns on both sides escorted us, a
cradling riff we were hoisted by.

Violin strings were Sedna's hair,
galloping bass was what untangled
                                     it,
cimbalom ligature ribs of a sunken
                                       ship,
conjunctive two to begin
with
gone

Batá drums what before had been
bass thrum. Batá horse-trot walked
us in... We tilted our heads back,
                                   put
drops in each eye. Anuncia disappeared...
                                   Boughs
    bent like bows now faded. He on whom her
tattoo'd lower back took aim faded. Anuncio,
    etc. No one cared... He and she were the
    last thing on our minds, we were in Quag,
                                   Quag's
    fish in a barrel shooting
    back

ANOUMAN SANDROFIA

—"mu" sixty-third part—

The crossroads bird he'd heard
sung about chirped all night. For
naught he'd have said but saved
   his breath, bemused how little it
                     came
to, to've been there but not known
it when… "Dear bird," he wanted
to say and so said it, want one side
                    of
   what soul was. "Dear bird," he
said, looking both ways. To've been
and been uncrossed couldn't be
thought he kept hearing the bird say,
                sing
   more what it was than say notwith-
standing, sing said more than say…
We the chorus insisted otherwise,
transmigration understood albeit
              not
   to say what soul was, soul itself
bruited between. He was looking
both ways and we were looking both
              ways,
   bird caught between as he and we
were caught between, Lone Coast
Ivory Coast… Spirit, we heard it
   say, not soul, three parts tremolo,
   two parts trill. We heard the bird
             he'd
   heard sung about sing, near side and
far side the same side, had we had our
   way every which way would've been
             how
it went… We the chorus remained un-
consoled. Bird, no bird, a million birds, no
matter, "Dear bird" some arrested prayer…
   No further walk… Momentary aspect…

Fleet, non-indigenous remit... The bird
he'd
heard sung about sang. Sign soon gone, in-
auspicious umbra. Sang but not for us we
insisted no end... Guitar clang escorted
bird clamor. He thought of crossroads
he'd
come to before... "Anouman Sandrofia"
commanded the night. The crossroads
bird he'd heard sung about said go
one
way or the other. One way, we said,
wasn't
enough

•

He stood listening having lain lament-
ing choices, lain serenaded by the
bird he'd heard sung about, stood all
but hearing us, all but not hearing
us,
up all night again like the night before...

Wile and regret before dawn broke. A
new world or an ultimate life night gave
new sense of, light each night kept lit
by irritant kin... Another's world if not
the
other world, world he was beckoned
by... Disenchanted canto, disconso-
late choir. Antiphonal rant we shot
back with... A conjunctive beak the com-
plaint we piped, a collaborative bird we
were
taken to be... The bird he'd heard sung
about sang and an answering bird not
sung about sang... Contrabass bird we sang,
semisang, raspy, gravelly, gruff. One way,
we
repeated, wasn't enough... Voice wasn't

enough, we sang ourselves hoarse, the
   contrabass bird nextet we now were,

never more exhortative than where we
   grew laconic, a cheap drumset in
                                    back
   of us, congas, bass guitar... An apo-
   retic sound ensemble we were, a we
                                    we
   would other-
wise be

•

Antibird, we sang like birds. Feathers
  left our mouths as we sang, we
  were cats... Nod house elysium
    rayed out from where the roads
                            met,
  nod house annexation, house turned
inside out... Chthonic porch. Side-
    real garden. Sugar met salt, salt
  sugar. Black cat collarbone spill...
  Warble a worm in our throats,
                        we
  talked birdtalk. Talked against birdtalk,
night, neck made of string. Night was
  asking where to next... Nowhere.
  Nothing. Nothingness. Gnosis put
                        salt
  on our tongues... Where was in
  sandrofia's beak he kept insisting,
    not-say he'd be instructed by. Trill
  was knowing not knowing, high light's
                            mod-
    ulated lament. Low light's antiphonal call
to itself, night lit by and by... As many
  in the ground as there were stars in the
                            sky,
    options by the millions by the wayside,
                                cross-
  roads burial mound... Options run out, run
  away from, whatever door he saw close
                            we
cracked

●

He stood on a ledge it seemed.
  Drowsily entwined what may
not have been there, night's
   all-knowing bereavement,
                  what
    might've come caught between...
Crossed as in crossed out, he'd
  lain awake thinking, world unreal,
   unregretful, hard head hard
   pillow's match. Brick squeeze,
                 nod
  house entablature... Guitar clang
   chimed all night... "Sad to say"
  said thru lips worn whisperless,
                we
  sang with big mouths never not
   open, lips drawn thin across our
                    teeth...
Utopic retort. Night's own embou-
  chure. Night's nextet, we came out
of nowhere, announcing and annulling the
  end of all things... All tack, all tone, all
                    inti-
  mation. Hummed as if words fell short.
  Stoic, post-ecstatic, not as if not knowing
                 them,
  him not even listening, heard us even so...
                  Bone
  we picked and picked at, ragalike picking
                no
  end

Picked it so it was a bone we
picked at, ragalike picking no
   end. Premature post-, pre-
emptive goodbye... Tell it
                              shut
up, we all but shouted, don't
   explain, bird he'd have been
   borne away by. High not his
                              to
be done with, above it all knowing
                                   what
   went
where

SONG OF THE ANDOUMBOULOU: 85

Came now to another crossroads.
Stick people stood awaiting us, to
the left, straight ahead, to the right.
    What was that song you sang,
                                    they
    asked, spoke without sound sound's
    immanence, not without song but
only one song, the one song summon-
ing song's eclipse... The one song
                                    sang
    song's inconsequence, crooned it
    could not've been otherwise, song
        song's own lament... The one
    song sang song's irrelevance, we
                                    were
    exhausted, we looked straight ahead,
                                    left,
    right. The stick people's question fa-
    tigued us, glyphed riddle whose
decipherment they said we'd someday
                                    be,
    exegetes against our will... Lack,
    reluctance, pallor, eidolon. Crossroads
cryptogram, they themselves were sing-
    ing, nothing not what could be seen they
                                    said,
    soul not sign if not eyelight, song more
    what could be seen than they could
    say, wan unwillingness they said... Slick
                                    stick
    people, tricky, soul a sick thing they said...
Signs all said Stick City. Stick City straight
    ahead, to the left, to the right, signs pointed
                                    every
    which way... Stick sublimity sent us reeling,
    a we that wasn't we against one that was. Mass,
intangible we it was we were, beads thrown off
    in a row... We'd have given anything to get to
                                    Stick
    City and there we were. Whatever way we

took would take us there. Stick City loomed
ahead and to the left and to the right, any which
way but in back of us, Stick City meant no
turning back... Signs all said Stick City. We
                                    read
    them all out loud, "Stick City." "Styxicity,"
                                            Itamar
    quipped... It wasn't water we crossed, it wasn't
    hell we were in. Stick City housed our hearts'
desires we were told, Stick City stood without
end or assistance, line long since what stuck...
                                            Line
        was all point, point all extensity, stick's own
    deictic drop... No longer point less point than
    point's target, Stick City made them one and the
same... So it was on to where the signs said next,
                                                Stick
        the one place we were yet to arrive at, Diddie Wa
    Diddie's twin. A winding road it now was we were
    on, so curved we could see our backs. No work,
    no worry up ahead we heard, music's utopic
                                            stir...
    Hogs lay stuck with knives and forks, chickens
    likewise we heard. A wall of beats for backup, Stick
                                                    City
    way off somewhere... As quick as that we were there,
Stick City. It wasn't the way we heard it was. Everyone
limped, walked with a cane, no way how we heard it
                                                was...
    As quick as that there we were. Stick City lay before
us, lied about. Legbaland it might've been... Diddie Wa
Diddie's non-identical twin if twin it was, no way the
                                                    way
    we heard it
    was

•

Stick-figure escorts ushered us in,
pointed out what was what. Stick
    people's gait was flawless, they
    said, unstick people limped on
                        sticks...
A strand of horsehair lay in the
    road, hair from a horse's tail. Come
rain it became a snake, would-be stick
                        though
        Stick City said no... It was getting
                        to
    be late again, the arcade's light less
    intense... Come night we lay under
        a horse, shouted voiceless trying
        to wake each other up and woke up,
                        coiled
    hair stiffened with earwax, as if at last
    we were Stick City's own... Not
so we saw soon enough. No home, no
    haven was it, noise what of it we could
                        keep...
    West L.A. it might've been, Saint-Pierre
    it might've been, wélélé no matter where
    we were... Stick symphony. Ictic sashay...
Head bob atop watery neck, nod homage,
                        noise,
    names came loose. What of it we kept we
        kept in name only, "Stick City" ours
        to hold on to. Chance it might've meant,
    I Ching, no place but we were long since
                        gone...
    Where sign had been sound X marked it,
    stick bisected stick. Signal some said, noise's
    alternate, half where we were nowhere near
                        where
we were, were where's discontent... It was getting
    to be light again, noise the new day's largesse.
    Sound was what sign turned out from, sound
        itself exed out... What the song was we sang
                        no

longer what we were asked, stick inquisitors
gathered, mum to the bone. Frown, furrowed
   brow, grimace the glyphs met us, faces
lined up in a row. Line was what pressed us,
     point egged us on, what the song was we
                        sang
   no song we sang, what the song was we sang
   moot... The strand-of-horsehair-become-a-snake
became a rope around our necks, rope what the
song we sang was. We'd have given anything
                     to
   say Stick City was where we were... Breath it
                   was
we gave, rope round our necks... We were neck-
less, bobbing heads, barbershop xtet, calabashes
   hit with sticks. Whatever we were, whatever
   noise there was we made ours. "This is our
dispatch," we said... Euphemistic necktie,
                  eu-
phemistic float. Horsehair tickling the tops
of our throats. Wet, euphemistic scruff... As it was
getting to be noon we got our necks and bodies
   back. A cartoon watch dog bit us, a pinscher
                with
   painted lips. We were stick people now, initiates.
                    Stick
legs only a blur, we were running, pant legs and hem-
lines ripped... Cross. Chiliasm. Crisis. Stick bisected
   stick. More hopeless the less we needed it, less
   real the more shot with stick vaccine, less real the
                 more
   stick we were... Stick inquisitors fell away as we went
   in. Stick City disappeared as we ran deeper. Too
   late to turn back, we were twigs, kindling, dispatch
                  gone
   up in smoke... We were jíbaros, hicks, cuatro ping
                 in
   back of us, howled, "Aylelolay lolelay." We stood
absorbed in what felt like advent. We stood on a plane
   cut thru an adverse cone. Low, rummaging burr, the
   sound we sought sought us, we the make-believe dead
                more

dead than we knew... Syllabic run was more alive than we
were, bass clack bugling disaster, brute sun outside the

nod

house door

Crossroads though it was it seemed an
impasse, stick as in stuck we thought. Stick
   as in stone's accomplice, Quag's bone-
      yard remit… Insofar as there was an
      I it fell in, a brass bell's everted lips
                                          now
   convergent, shush we were hollowed by.
Insofar as there was an I it was as each of us
      insisted, as far as there was an I, stick
      beating stick, there was an X… Crux…
                                    Cross…
      Crutch… Legs' Osirian soulstrut lost,
   Legbaland it was and we limped on, limped
      in, Stick City's outskirts endless it
      seemed, no matter we leaned on sticks…
                                          Were
      there an I it stood like a stick, mum-stuff
         crossing itself. Insofar as there was
      an I it was an X taking shape, there but
to be gone if not no sooner there than gone,
                                          glass
      house holding
   its own

We knew we wore skeleton suits. We knew
we walked holding placards. "Dead from
   Day One" they read, part requiem, part
rebuke… What lay around us had the
                                    sound
   of steam. Low-motion lurk. Time-lapse cascade.
   Stick City city limits notwithstanding, glass
intangibles allowed what was lost otherwise,
                                          gripless
      in the house outside the house… It slipped
   away and we slipped away and it slipped away,
                                             Stick
      City a mirage nod concocted, not to be be-
   lieved but we did though it receded, nod Nub's
                                             emic
      retreat